CAMPAIGN FURNITURE

GULF

OF

EXICO

Charlotte Harbor

FLORIDA

GUL... STREAM

Galapagos Keys

Guana K?

Gr. Bahama I.

Benim Is.

Sberrys Is.

New Providence

Nassau

Cape Sable

STRAIT OF FLORIDA

Tortugas Is.

Key West

FLORIDA REEFS

Harbor Islands

Salt Keys

GREAT

BAHAMA

B?

Bahia Honda

Guanajai

HAVANA

Matanzas

Cardenas

Sagua la Grande

Organos Pt

Batabano

Cape Antonio

ISLA

Bejucal

New Gerona

Broad B.

Cienfuegos

Santa Clara

Remedios

Cayos

Romano

Isle of Pines

Cayo Large

Trinidad

Espiritu Santo

N D

OF

C U

Negulo B.

Puerto Principe

YUCATAN

Buena Esperanza B

Little Cayman

Cape de Cruz

GRE

Grand Cayman

C

CARIB

G R

JAMAI

Falmouth

Blue M?s

South Negril Pt

8,184

Savana la Mar

SPANISH TOWN

Black River

A

I

B

CAMPAIGN FURNITURE

BY CHRISTOPHER SCHWARZ

Abaco I.

HA

euthera

Guanahani or St. Salvador I.
The first part of America discovered by
Columbus.
Watling I.

I S L A N D S

Tropic of Cancer

Long I.   Atwood I.

Jumentos
Is

Crooked Is

Mariguana

Acklin I.

West Caycos   Great Caycos I.

Mila's Pt.   Grand Inagua   Caycos Is   Turk's Islands

el Cobre   T E R   A N T I L L

Baracoa   Passage

T. Maysi   Tortuga I   Port Platte   Scott's B.

Windward   Cape Haytien   Cibao Mts   Samana B.
Passage   8.600

Gonaives   Artibonite R.   D O M I N I C A

Gonaive   Salt   Azua   St
                             Lake   DOMINGO

tonio   Jereme   H A I T I   C. Engano

C. Tiburon   PORT AUPRINCE   Froa B.

rant Pt.   Aux Cayes   Jacmel   False C.   Beata

I S L A N D   O F   H A Y T I

E   A   N   S

Published by Lost Art Press LLC in 2014
26 Greenbriar Ave., Fort Mitchell, KY 41017, USA
Web: http://lostartpress.com

Title: Campaign Furniture
Author: Christopher Schwarz
Editor: Megan Fitzpatrick
Acquisition Editor: John Hoffman
Index: Suzanne Ellison

This book was printed and bound in the United States of America.

CONTENTS

Preface…vii

1. CAMPAIGN STYLE   1
2. CAMPAIGN WOODS   38
3. CAMPAIGN HARDWARE   52
4. CAMPAIGN CHESTS   82
5. CAMPAIGN SECRETARIES   122
6. FOLDING CAMP STOOL   138
7. ROORKEE CHAIRS   154
8. STRONG TRUNK   190
9. FIELD DESK   214
10. COLLAPSIBLE BOOKSHELVES   234
11. TRAVELING BOOKCASE   248

Afterword… 265
Appendices
A. ROUBO ON CAMPAIGNING… 269
B. INDIA'S JOINERS, BY GEORGE CECIL… 279
C. ARMY & NAVY STORES… 285
Acknowledgements…318
Further Reading…319
Index…323
Hardware Sources…331

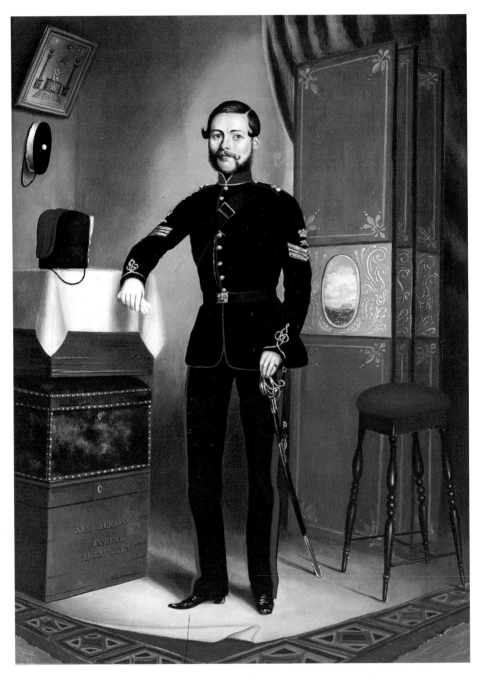

FIG. 1. "Sgt. J. Craig," an oil on canvas by an unknown artist, circa 1870.
(Courtesy of the Council of the National Army Museum, London)

Rear Rank Firing

PREFACE

RUGGED & SIMPLE

Like a dormant case of malaria, my fevered love for campaign furniture began many years ago without my knowledge – probably during some hot Connecticut summer.

My maternal grandparents' home (and ours) was full of campaign furniture. When you drank tea with grandmother West, it was on a folding coaching table my grandfather had built. My grandfather, an enthusiastic woodworker, had brought back campaign brasses from his trips to Asia, some of which I still own. So his pieces definitely had an Anglo-Indian campaign feel to them. And when you visited the West's house for the summer, you put your clothes in a campaign chest.

My father and mother were fond of the furniture as well. And when my dad built pieces for our home they were at times festooned with brass corner guards, brackets and flush-mount pulls.

As a child, I didn't think much of the provenance of all this furniture. In fact, I assumed it was Chinese or Japanese furniture because my grandparent's house was also awash in tansu, Chinese chests and ink paintings of landscapes and animals.

Eventually I wised up and sorted out the furniture record of all our households. The campaign style became a favorite of mine, and I wanted to build pieces of it for the magazine I worked for at the time, *Popular Woodworking*.

My fellow editors, however, were inoculated against the bug. There was almost nothing written about the style of furniture. And whenever we surveyed our readership, subscribers told us that there were three furniture styles they preferred: country (anything with a duck or pineapple on it), Shaker and Arts & Crafts. "Campaign furniture" was somewhere down the list near "narwhal nose guards" in popularity.

I persisted. I was rejected again. And after I stepped down as editor in 2011, I asked them one last time to publish two articles – one on campaign chests and a second on Roorkee chairs. After some wrangling and veiled threats, they said OK.

That was the start of my obsession with researching and building campaign furniture. Since 2010, I have been neck-deep in researching the style of furniture that I cannot remember living without. During the last 200 years, there has been surprisingly little written about campaign furniture, which also goes by the name of "barracks furniture," "camp furniture" or sometimes "patent furniture." There's an excellent book by Nicholas A. Brawer that is the single reference work for collectors and dealers, but it is out of print. Plus there are some magazine articles.

Most of the knowledge out there on campaign furniture is in the hands of auctioneers, antique dealers and restorers. So my research began with their sales records, and that led me to the catalogs of the British furniture makers of the 19th and early 20th centuries. Plus I dug up several helpful 19th-century books that sought to prepare a British citizen for a long trip abroad.

The real surprise from my initial research was that these pieces of beautiful "military" furniture weren't just for the military. With the incredible expansion of the British Empire in the 19th century, there was an urgent need for a bureaucracy to manage the Empire's colonies. (Brawer writes in his book that by 1897 the British Empire comprised one-quarter of the world's land surface.)

So these campaign chests, folding tables, collapsible chairs and writing desks were in use by bureaucrats, writers, doctors, merchants – plus their families – all over the globe.

Even more interesting: The knockdown aspect of the furniture made it popular with city dwellers who were crammed into tiny city flats – it allowed them to convert a parlor to a dining room to a bedroom. And if you left England on a ship to colonize an island, such as New Zealand, this type of furniture filled your stateroom during the journey and your home when you arrived.

Oh, and if you were a student who left home to go to school, you might tote along some of these items, such as a folding bookcase and a writing slope.

In fact, the romantic idea that all of these pieces of campaign furniture were portaged on the backs of elephants through the jungle is mostly off the mark. In truth, most of these pieces of furniture were the workaday backbone of furniture for people who needed stuff that was rugged, simple and a bit stylish.

And that idea – rugged, simple and stylish furniture – is what kept me coming back to the belief that campaign furniture is a sorely underappreciated furniture form.

As a woodworker, I love the first-class joinery: dovetails plus mortise-and-tenon joints. The simple and rectilinear lines are easy for beginners to make and are as familiar as Shaker or Arts & Crafts items. If you're not a woodworker, I hope you can appreciate the simple forms and clean lines that look good in almost any room, whether you fill your rooms with 18th-century stuff or Bauhaus. Campaign furniture fits in everywhere, across the globe and in every time period.

I think that's true in part because it was truly an international furniture style. The roots of the style might indeed be related to tansu, as some have suggested, or in Chinese traveling forms, as others contend. But what is certain is that when Asian craftsmen saw these British forms they reinterpreted them for their customers. When their customers took these pieces back to England, the cabinetmakers there were influenced by the changes made by their far-flung brothers. And so forth and so on.

When I finally made that last connection to that circle, I didn't feel so stupid about assuming that my grandparents' campaign furniture was from Asia.

It is my hope that this book opens your eyes to a style of furniture that was around for about 200 years – 1740 to World War II by some reckonings – and remains sturdy and stylish (if somewhat underappreciated) today.

This book is not an academic investigation of this furniture style – I will leave that desperately needed task to more capable researchers. Instead, this book is a too-short look at the furniture style from a builder's perspective. My interest is in the wood, the hardware, the joinery and the different forms themselves.

I think that if you put your hand to building these pieces to the high standards of the 18th and 19th centuries, you will become fascinated – might I say "infected" – by their cleverness and soundness of construction.

Campaign furniture was meant to endure a mobile existence and do it with a bit of grace. To be sure, we are a more mobile society now than we were 200 years ago and sorely need furniture that is easy to move. And if you have bought any furniture in the last 50 years, you also know that most factory furniture is doomed to self-destruct within a few years.

We need campaign furniture more than ever before. Fill your house with it, and the ideals it embodies – sturdiness, simplicity and beauty – might just seep into the unconscious minds of your children or grandchildren as it did for me.

Christopher Schwarz
Fort Mitchell, Kentucky
January 2014

Fig. 1.1. "The Hero of Lucknow." An engraving by A. H. Ritchie of General Sir Henry Havelock seated in an X-frame chair at a desk, which is covered with a cloth. Note the trunk at his feet. (Courtesy of the Council of the National Army Museum, London)

CHAPTER 1

CAMPAIGN STYLE

The term "campaign furniture" is usually applied to a wide range of pieces were produced for British citizens living abroad between the middle of the 18th century to the middle of the 20th.

What we now call campaign furniture was produced during a dizzying number of English furniture periods and sub-periods. Pieces of this particular ilk were first made during the Georgian era (1714-1837), a period that encompasses designs from the pattern books of Thomas Chippendale, Robert and James Adam, George Hepplewhite and Thomas Sheraton.

Campaign furniture continued to blossom during the Regency (1810-1820) and Victorian (1837-1901) periods – the height of the British Empire. Only in the early 20th century did the campaign style begin to decline as the Empire and the needs of its military changed. Most accounts of campaign furniture peg its official demise as somewhere in the mid-20th century.

What is most remarkable about this incredibly long run for the campaign style is how consistent many of its core designs remained. Changes during the decades were subtle when contrasted to the large lurches and stylistic swings seen in the high styles of Chinese Chippendale, neoclassicism, the Gothic revival and rococo (to name a few).

Figs. 1.2 & 1.3 The Georgian Navy. A small-sized naval bureau in mahogany, circa 1750-80 (Georgian period). The drawers are lined with cedar. Lifts on the ends were likely as much for tying the bureau down during rough seas as moving it. Dimensions: 37-1/2" H x 27-3/4" W x 16-1/2" D. (Courtesy of Christopher Clarke Antiques)

A campaign chest from the late 18th century, for example, is remarkably similar to one from 1929. True, there are clues from the hardware and feet that make it straightforward to distinguish one from the other, but most lay people would be hard-pressed to date either one.

Even with dining tables and chairs, which usually respond quickly to changes in style, stylistic details were somewhat muted when produced for travelers, sea captains or army officers.

The reason for this conservatism might have something to do with the fact that military officers were the most important customers for the furniture makers. (Military tastes are usually conservative.) But more important, in my opinion, is that campaign pieces were intended for traveling. So they had to be, above all else, rugged and well made without delicate ornament, such as carvings or mouldings.

So while inlay, stringing and banding were popular during the Regency period (concurrent with what Americans call the Federal period), these ornaments were not practical for a chest of drawers that had to be packed tightly inside a second packing box and shipped to India, the Indies, Africa or New Zealand.

Sean Clarke, one of the owners of Christopher Clarke Antiques in Gloucestershire, put it this way during an interview:

"I think there's quite a strong theory with chests and earlier campaign furniture that an officer might go to a local cabinetmaker who has a pattern book. The officer would say, 'I like that piece, but I need to make it to travel. Remove moulding, split it in two and so forth.'"

Origins of the Style

Sean Clarke and his brother, Simon, have spent an enormous amount of energy researching the makers, users and history of campaign furniture pieces in order to publish their catalogs, which are intended to sell campaign pieces, but are also a fantastic vein of research.

The Clarkes suspect that many of the ideas behind British campaign furniture evolved from furniture used by Chinese government officials as part of that country's mobile government. The Clarkes discount the idea of Japanese tansu as being a direct source of inspiration for British campaign furniture. Japan, they point out, was largely closed to foreigners until 1853, well after the development of the campaign style.

The Clarkes see campaign pieces such as the chest of drawers as a close descendant of Georgian chests, some of which could be broken down into two or three pieces for travel. And they have handled enough Georgian and campaign pieces to make the point convincingly.

The 18th-century furniture was likely bespoke for the most part, Sean Clarke says. Officers had to purchase their commission in the military and outfit themselves at their own expense, including purchasing their traveling furniture.

Figs. 1.4 &1.5 Another early chest. The reeding and cockbeading indicate this chest is circa 1800. What is fascinating about this form is that even though its secretary mechanism is unusual, the assembled chest still looks very much like the classic campaign chest. In mahogany with ebony cockbeading. Dimensions: 30" H x 38-3/4" W x 20-1/2" D. (Courtesy of Christopher Clarke Antiques)

As the British Empire expanded and the Napoleonic wars dawned in the early 19th century, several manufacturers began to specialize in making campaign furniture for the military and travelers, and designs became more standardized. This trend continued throughout the 19th century as more firms began to specialize in outfitting those going abroad. By the late 19th century, Brawer estimates there were at least 85 makers and designers of campaign furniture in the London area alone, according to an article he wrote for *The Magazine Antiques* (September 2000).

Figs. 1.6 & 1.7 Catalog chest. This late-19th century secretary (Victorian period) is found in the Army & Navy Co-operative Society catalog. The piece was available in the 1907 catalog in teak, oak or mahogany, with mahogany being the most expensive. The chest features a secret drawer. Dimensions: 44" H x 39" W x 19-3/4" D. (Courtesy of Christopher Clarke Antiques)

Figs. 1.8 & 1.9 Early secretary. Another early mahogany chest – note the skeleton-ized pulls, the moulded top edge and the lack of brass strapping. This chest, circa 1800, was built by Ramsey & Co. Dimensions: 39-3/4" H x 39-1/2" W x 20-1/2" D. (Courtesy of Christopher Clarke Antiques)

Figs. 1.10 & 1.11 Regency chest. Even later chests, such as this circa 1820 Regency example, weren't immune to changes in furniture style. Note the reeding throughout and the inset brass pulls that closely resemble traditional swan's neck pulls. (Courtesy of Christopher Clarke Antiques)

Fig. 1.12 Patent chair. This mahogany library chair with a caned seat is very similar to one made by Morgan & Sanders in the early 19th century.

Patent Furniture

The growth of campaign furniture during the early 19th century coincided with another furniture trend that was related, but separate. Patent furniture – also called "metamorphic" furniture – was the rage during the Regency period. Patent furniture was, at its core, somewhat mechanical. Chairs, desks, beds and sofas all transformed into another form of furniture. The cleverest designs were granted patents – hence the name.

Many firms that made patent furniture also made campaign furniture, such as the firms of Morgan & Sanders (1801-1820), Thomas Butler (1787-1814) and Thomas & Samuel Oxenham (1795-1832), according to Brawer. And so it is no surprise that this sort of technology spilled over into the lines of furniture intended for travelers.

By the middle of the 19th century, even the handbooks for travelers would regularly recommend buying metamorphic furniture for a journey.

The passage being engaged, and the average price, eighty pounds, duly paid, the next object which engages attention is the purchase of cabin furniture and the outfit. In the selection of these, the passenger will be prudent always to keep in mind the possibility of converting them to useful purposes in India. Thus, a sofa with drawers beneath it, is preferable to a swing-cot, because it can be rendered serviceable in a house, whereas the uses of the latter terminate with the voyage.

– "The Handbook of British India: A Guide to the Stranger, the Traveller, the Resident…" by J.H. Stocqueler (Wm. H. Allen, 1854)

Figs. 1.13 & 1.14 Late Victorian card table. This folding card table, one of my favorite mechanical pieces, folds flat into a remarkably small box. The clever mechanism shows that long after the patent furniture craze cooled in the early 19th century, the technology was still useful. Dimensions: 27" H x 21 7/8" W x 22" D. (Courtesy of Christopher Clarke Antiques)

So even after the passion for patent furniture faded amongst the general public, the ideas were carried forward and refined for the traveling pieces built for the Victorians.

Victorian Campaign Furniture

The Victorian era (1837-1901) is considered the height of the British Empire, but it is a period usually ignored by modern woodworkers, except as a foil to the British and American Arts & Crafts movements.

That's unfortunate, because it was a period of remarkable productivity and ingenuity among furniture makers, especially when it came to campaign furniture.

During the Victorian era, Britain's population almost doubled, a strong middle class developed, cities became overcrowded and the Empire expanded to almost every corner of the world. All of these changes made campaign furniture an

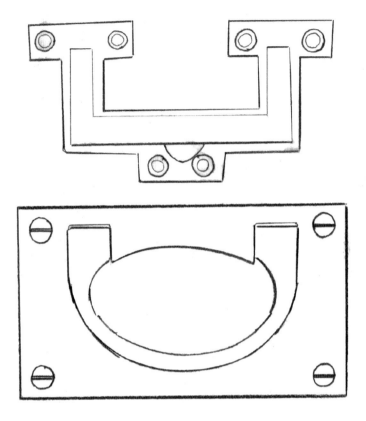

Figs. 1.15 & 1.16 Early & late. Skeletonized pulls (top) are more difficult to install than later ones (bottom) with a rectangular backplate.

important part of the furniture- and trunk-making industries.

The new middle class had money to spend on education, leisure and sport; people packed into small flats needed furniture that could be stashed away; and British citizens were traveling all over as they administered the Empire and its interests.

The British-made campaign furniture of this period assumed a fairly standard set of brasses. The pulls were still recessed, of course, but they were in many ways simpler. The earlier "skeletonized" brasses resembled the typical swan's neck pulls of the 19th century. The Victorian pulls had a rectangular backplate – usually with coves at the corners.

In addition to the pulls, later casework was built with more brass guards at the corners. Some pieces were bound in an astonishing amount of brass.

The flush hardware has always been a source of fascination for me as a builder. Adding the inset hardware adds 20 to 30 percent more labor to a piece in comparison to one that uses surface-mounted pulls. So something about the flush hardware was key. To be sure, some of it was fashion. Earlier campaign pieces didn't incorporate as many bits of hardware compared to later pieces.

And flush hardware also was a mark of quality. Many campaign pieces produced in India would use brass fittings that were thin metal, not mortised into the wood and secured with nails instead of screws.

Sean Clarke noted that the flush hardware allowed casework to slide into tightly fitted traveling boxes. And, of course, furniture with flush hardware can be packed more closely than furniture with surface-mounted hardware.

As a builder, I suspect the guards also protected the pieces from the specific dangers of the tropics. Animal-based adhesives of the time were susceptible to heat, water and insects – all three of which could be encountered on any given day in the colonies.

The brass guards, with the assistance of their screws, made the joinery inherently stronger. Even if the hide-based glue failed due to exposure to heat, bugs or water, the brass fasteners and guards served to keep the piece together.

So relaxed did the glue become by the humidity of the atmosphere, that every article of furniture dropped to pieces; and many a bachelor, whose clamped and strong camp-furniture effectually defied these devastating effects of the climate, and consequently enabled him to lounge securely at home, has made a ludicrous appearance when he has incautiously thrown himself back in the more light and elegant furniture of his married companions…. Woe unto such as in the pride of their hearts had brought over beaded or veneered furniture! Every ornament gradually and silently dropped off….

– *"The Asiatic Journal and Monthly Register for British India and its Dependencies," Vol. 26, July to December 1828 (Parbury, Allen, & Co.)*

At the end of the Victorian era, the world of campaign furniture changed rapidly because of two events. First was the rise of the Army & Navy Co-operative Society Ltd., which was founded in 1871 and became a one-stop department store for its members traveling abroad. The Society sold everything, from tools to wine to furniture to lamps and jewelry – even an evening's entertainment.

The Society eventually replaced the manufacturers of campaign furniture and became the chief supplier of goods to military officers and other travelers. Using the Society's catalog, you could order almost anything to be delivered anywhere from one of the company's offices all over the world. (The company still does business as House of Fraser.)

The other change to campaign furniture came about because of the Second Boer War (1899-1902), where the British were outmaneuvered in South Africa by the swiftly moving Boer forces. The expensive, long and unpopular war led to

Fig. 1.17 Tough on furniture. "The Chetta Ravine, Abyssinia, 1868," by Lt. Cornelius Francis. This watercolor shows an expeditionary force passing through the Chetta Ravine to reach Magdala. Note the unruly pack animals and their loads. (Courtesy of the Council of the National Army Museum, London)

the British military sloughing off its tradition of carrying along a small British city behind it wherever it went.

While many heavy and bulky campaign furniture forms became obsolete as a result, new forms were developed. One of the most notable was the Roorkee chair, a lightweight and portable chair that influenced generations of furniture designers and is an important link between the late Victorians and early modernism.

During the first part of the 20th century, campaign forms were still manufactured, though the selection became smaller in the Army & Navy catalog year by year. During my research, I have dug up campaign brasses that were manufactured during the late 1950s, and there are still campaign brasses being made today, many of them unchanged from the mid-19th century.

So in some ways, campaign furniture has never gone away. The style has experienced a few minor resurgences since World War II. Even now you'll see new furniture pieces that are bristling with brass corner guards and flush pulls (but are made from chipboard that's poked with screws). But as you'll see in this book, campaign furniture is more than just an exotic veneer and flush brass.

Quality campaign furniture – no matter what the period – was built to last. It is furniture that has been stripped of excess ornament (so it looks at home in any period). It has been built with top-shelf joinery that is reinforced with brass hardware (so it is almost indestructible). And it is made from the best materials – good quality walnut, oak, mahogany, camphor or teak (so it is inherently beautiful).

If you embark on building a campaign piece, I urge you to carry on with these same principles. Purchase the best lumber and brasses available. Do not cut corners on joinery, fasteners, adhesive or finish. Build the piece so it could cross the Chetta Ravine, get dropped by a pack animal and still survive. Only then will you truly gain an appreciation for the original makers of these ingenious pieces.

Fig. 1.18 Three-tiered chest. This campaign chest is unusual in that it is composed of three separate units instead of the typical two. According to the National Army Museum, John Nicholson (1821-1857) owned the chest. He was first commissioned into the Bengal Infantry in 1839 and spent his entire career in India. (Courtesy of the Council of the National Army Museum, London)

Figs. 1.19 & 1.20 The spectrum of the style. An early campaign chest (left), and a much later Victorian chest.

A Field Guide to the Classic Campaign Pieces

Once you start looking for campaign pieces at antique stores and in museums, you likely will be surprised by how many are out there – even in the United States. What follows is a quick-and-dirty guide to some of the common forms and their construction details.

Campaign Chests

Brass-bound campaign chests that can be split into two parts are likely the most iconic pieces of the style – like the Morris chair of the Arts & Crafts movement. The archetypal British-made chest is mahogany with four rows of drawers, brass corner guards and flush brass pulls. Most chests would fit nicely into a box that is 40" H x 40" W x 22" D.

However, there are lots of variants of campaign chests and details about their construction that you should consider as a maker when you plan to build your own. The following details apply to British-made chests. Campaign chests made in China or India are outside the scope of this book.

As far as dating the chests, a good rule of thumb is that earlier chests had fewer brass corner guards and used pulls that are "skeletonized." That is, the early pulls look more like the classic swan's neck type. In addition to the skeletonized pulls, there are also some early pulls that have pointed ends and other shapes. Early chests are also more likely to have moulding than a later chest, though the ornament is usually more subdued than that on a high-style chest for domestic use.

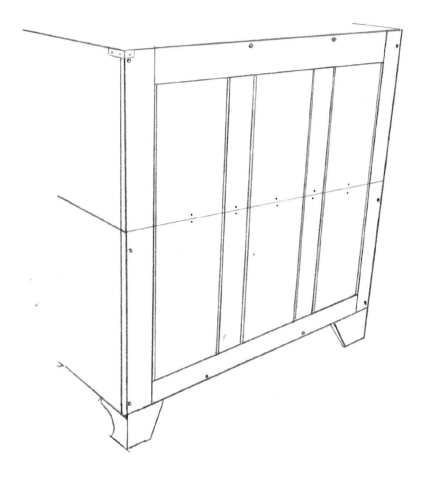

Fig. 1.21 Paneled back. The frame of this back stiffens the carcases. The thin interior panels reduce the weight. These backs are more work to construct than a simple boarded back.

Because early chests were more likely made as one-off pieces (and not in a manufactory), you are apt to see more variation in their design and construction. So you can encounter (or use) almost any joinery variant of the dovetail family.

Later chests in the mid-19th century became more standardized. More brass was added. The pulls became rectangular and fairly uniform among the manufacturers. From a builder's perspective, these later chests are well built and are worth studying and reproducing.

Here are some other construction details of the chests, both early and late.

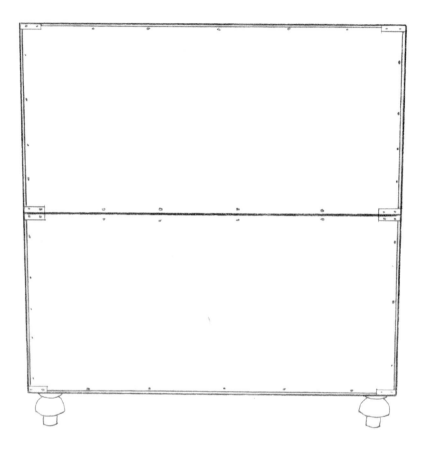

Fig. 1.22 Boarded back. This common form of back has the panels screwed into rabbets in the carcases. It is not as robust as a typical frame-and-panel assembly, but it is quick to execute. The grain typically runs horizontal on the backboards.

Backs of Campaign Chests

The backs of campaign chests can run the full gamut of techniques. I've seen frame-and-panel backs all the way down to backs that were simply nailed into a rabbet in the rear of the carcase.

A frame-and-panel back is by far the lightest in weight (because of the thin panels) and adds the most rigidity to the carcase, which is a frameless cabinet that benefits from the rigidity. You'll also see backs that were paneled (usually via tongue-and-groove) and simple full panels that are inset into a rabbet or a groove. These options are preferred to a simple nailed- or screwed-on back.

Fig. 1.23 Half-blinds. The top board of the lower case that is joined to one of the ends. When the two components of the chest are stacked on top of one another, the tails are concealed.

Corner Joinery

When it comes to the joinery, most of these chests were dovetailed at the corners. Except for the very top board of the cases (which were joined with full-blind dovetails), the remaining tops and bottoms were typically joined to the ends with half-blind (also called lap) dovetails.

On all the examples I've examined so far, the tail boards have been on the tops and bottoms, and the pin boards are on the ends of the carcases. This violates the typical practice of putting the tails on the end boards, which makes the joints stronger for lifting.

Figs. 1.24 & 1.25 Full-blind dovetails. The two components of a full-blind dovetail construction. When these two parts are driven together, you cannot see the tails or the pins.

My guess is that this is for simplicity's sake. With the tails on the tops and bottoms, these joints are laid out and executed exactly like cutting the joints for a drawer. If you put the tails on the end boards, removing the waste in the blind tails would be a little more difficult. But most of all, it would be a less-common way of cutting the joint.

The tops of campaign chests were typically joined to the ends with rabbeted full-blind dovetails. Details of this joint are covered in the chapter on building campaign chests. After pulling the drawers out of a number of these chests and poking around with a flashlight, I've found that for this joint, it was typical to put the tails on the end boards and the pins on the top. (You can easily discern this in a glued-up joint by paying attention to the overcuts from the dovetail saw and if they are angled or vertical.)

Sometimes the corners of the carcases will be joined with through-dovetails, though I haven't seen many of these in the wild or in auction catalogs. There are also a few chests where all the joints are half-blind dovetails and you can see the tails on the top.

Interior Joinery

Because these chests have to be strong, the interiors are usually mortise-and-tenon web frames with dust panels – again, first-class joinery. I've seen a few chests where the interior dividers are solid slab panels. These are simpler to build, but the slabs add weight.

The web frames are usually attached to the end boards with dados or, in some cases, sliding dovetails. You can tell which joint the maker used by removing the brass corner guards covering them.

As far as attaching the top case to the bottom case, it is typically done with two to four dowels that stick up on one of the cases and slide into matching holes in the other case. There are other methods of registering the top case to the bottom,

Fig. 1.26 Inside a chest. You can see the web frame and dust panel inside this vintage campaign chest. Also, note the locations of the drawer stops, which keep the drawer front flush to the frame of the carcase.

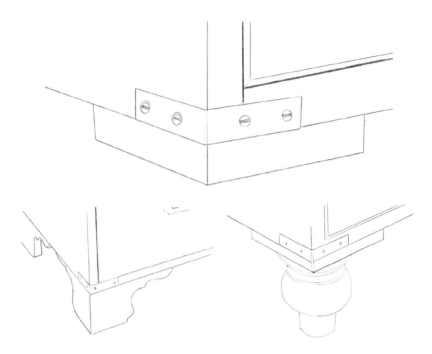

Fig. 1.27 A sledge foot, bracket foot and turned foot.

including brass hardware that is incorporated into the corner guards, but I haven't seen enough of these to know which other methods are typical and which are not.

Other Details

The plinth, or base, of a campaign chest is almost always one of three constructions: turned feet that unscrew from the lower carcase for traveling, a traditional bracket foot (some of these feet were added later in the chest's life) or a "sledge" foot – just a square pad at each corner. Note that sometimes these sledge feet are on chests that are missing their original turned feet.

Chests built for the Navy sometimes have different features. Sean Clarke says that chests that have a short three-sided gallery on their tops were likely for the Navy. The raised lip prevented items from sliding off the top during the voyage.

Also, naval chests might have handles on the ends of the carcases. While these handles were probably used to lift the sections while moving the chest, they also were designed to lash the chests to the deck of the ship. Sean Clarke notes that some antique dealers will add these handles to a campaign chest thinking they look "more proper" when they are not.

Most chests designed for the Army would not have these lifts because the chest had to slide into a tightly fitted case.

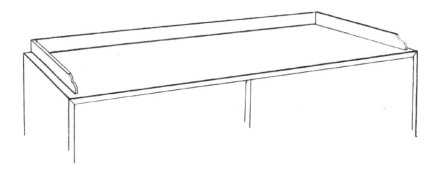

Fig. 1.28 A gallery on a naval chest.

Fig. 1.29 A rare find. The wooden cases that protected campaign chests are quite rare these days. The exterior case could be used as a wardrobe when you got to your destination and removed the chest of drawers. (Courtesy of Christopher Clarke Antiques)

Campaign Secretaries

A fair number of these chests turn up with some sort of integral writing surface, from a simple writing slope that gets propped up from a drawer, to a full-blown drop-front with a gallery and secret drawers. The secretary section of the chest could be located in one of several places: the entire full-width top or second-row drawer, a center drawer that is flanked by two smaller drawers, or one of the two smaller drawers in the top row of drawers.

No. 8. With middle escritoire, 3 ft. 3
in. long, 1 ft. 7 in. wide, and 3 ft. 7
in. high; secretary drawer 8¼ in.
deep, 2 small drawers 8¼ in. deep,
1 drawer 7¼ in. deep, 1 drawer 4¾
in. deep, 1 drawer 10½ in. deep.
Teak £10 13 9
Do., mahogany 10 18 3
Do., oak 10 6 6

No. 3a. Set of drawers, with table escritoire, but without shelves and
fittings, size 3 ft. 3 in. long, 1 ft. 8
in. wide, 3 ft. 9 in. high. 2 drawers
5¾ in. deep, 1 drawer 7 in. deep,
escritoire 4½ in. deep, 1 drawer
5¾ in. deep, 1 drawer 10½ in.
deep. This chest is fitted with
secret drawer. Teak £12 16 6
Do., oak 12 13 6
Do., mahogany 13 1 6

No. 10. Chest with long escritoire, 3 ft.
3 in. long, 1 ft. 7 in. wide, 3 ft. 7 in.
high, escritoire 8 in. deep. One
drawer 4½ in. deep, 1 drawer 8 in.
deep, 1 drawer 10½ in. deep. Teak £11 10 3
Do., mahogany 11 10 3
Do., oak 11 5 6

No. 7. Chest with side escritoire, 3 ft.
3 in. long. 1 ft. 6 in. wide, and 3 ft.
5 in. high, 2 drawers 8 in. deep, 1
drawer 7½ in. deep, 1 drawer 4 in.
deep, 1 drawer 10 in. deep. Teak £9 10 6
Do. mahogany 9 14 3
Do. oak 9 7 9

Fig. 1.30 A sample of secretaries carried by the Army & Navy Co-operative Society.

Cases for Chests of Drawers.

Cases for military chests of drawers, painted,
iron bound, and fitted with sunk handles.
For Chests No. 2, 3, 4, and 4a........ £4 14 9
    ,,   ,, 3a 4 0 3
    ,,   ,, 5 and 7................. 3 12 3
    ,,   ,, 8, 9 and 10 .... 3 14 6

Fig. 1.31 Cases for a campaign chest.

Fig. 1.32 A Chinese-made secretary.

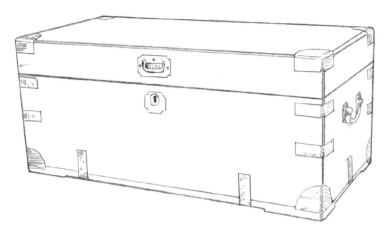

Fig. 1.33 A typical campaign trunk.

Strong Trunks

Campaign trunks, what we might call a footlocker or floor chest, are almost as common as campaign chests (at least among pieces that have made it to the United States). Trunks are fairly similar in both size (34" W x 20" H x 20" D) and in construction, with the differences being in the details and the woods.

The Army & Navy Co-Operative Society catalog carried a wide variety of these trunks that could be made in anything from deal (a white softwood) up to a mahogany version that could be lined in zinc, camphor or cedar.

The catalog offered the Midshipman's Sea Chest, which had a sliding till and two trays, one that can be used as a washstand, plus a mirror, candle sconce and your name engraved on a brass plate affixed to the chest's exterior.

"Strong Chests for Travelling" were made from "good seasoned wood" and were bound in iron and painted. This chest was available as the No. 13 Strong Barrack Chest fitted with a Bramah lock and lined with green baize.

If you were an officer or going to India, the Army & Navy Co-operative Society catalog recommended zinc-lined chests, which were "approximately air tight." And if you were in the Army, you were steered to the Regulation Army Chests, which also were zinc-lined.

No matter what chest you purchased, you could have your name and regiment painted on the chest for a shilling. Or just your initials for 2 pennies.

Most of the trunks I have encountered in the wild are dovetailed at the corners – tails on the front and back, with pins on the ends. The interiors are usually plain and unfinished; sometimes there is a small till at one end like you would find in a typical blanket chest.

Regulation Army Chests.

With sunk handles, as sealed pattern.

		Zinc lined.
1. 3 ft. 6 in. by 2 ft. 2 in. by 2 ft.	£3 5 9	£3 18 6
2. 3 ft. 4 in. by 1 ft. 10 in. by 1 ft. 8 in.	2 17 9	3 8 0
3. 2 ft. 6 in. by 2 ft. by 1 ft.	2 0 6	2 7 9
4. 2 ft. 2 in. by 1 ft. 2 in. by 1 ft.	1 8 3	1 13 0

No. 13. Strong Barrack Chest, iron bound and painted, to hold sundries, size 3 ft. by 1 ft. 8 in. by 1 ft. 8 in. £1 13 3

Do. do. lined with green baize and fitted with Bramah lock, for use as plate chest 2 19 3

Storage Boxes.

Outside stained and clamped with lock, and two countersunk screws in lid.

These boxes are designed to meet a demand for a strong but inexpensive chest, suited for travelling, storage of goods, plate, &c.

Outside measurement—	No. 1 size.	No. 2 size.	No. 3 size.
	27 by 20½ by 16.	31 by 22½ by 19.	38 by 29 by 17½
Quite plain inside ...	21/0	23/9	27/6
Do., with wooden tray	25/6	29/0	34/9
Zinc lined	29/9	33/6	37/9
Do., with wooden tray	34/3	38/9	45/0
Green baize lined ...	30/6	35/0	38/6
Do., with wooden tray	42/6	47/0	50/3

Strong Chests for Travelling.
(Of good seasoned wood.)

No. 12. Strong Sea Chest, 3 ft. by 1 ft. 7 in. by 1 ft. 8 in., iron bound and painted £1 7 0
Fitted with a 6-in. tray 1 12 9

Fig. 1.34 A sample of trunks carried by the Army & Navy Co-operative Society.

Figs. 1.35, 1.36 & 1.37 Mahogany-like trunk. This typical trunk is built using mahogany (or a dendrological cousin). Despite the nice wood and dovetailed corners, the brass corner guards are applied (not flush) and are nailed on.

The top and bottom of the chest are typically applied to the carcase or rabbeted into the carcase, though sometimes you will find the top and bottom floating in a groove. Inside the trunk, the top and bottom are sometimes reinforced with a center muntin or even a few muntins.

As to the base, I've seen three typical arrangements: a small sledge base, a small bracket foot and (sometimes) no base at all. The sledge base is, in my experience, the most common form.

In addition to the brass corner guards, trunks usually had lifts – either brass or iron – on the ends. The front of the lid typically had a single recessed pull to make it easier to lift the lid after unlocking the trunk. And don't forget a lock or a hasp.

Fig. 1.38 Painted trunk. Another exotic-wood trunk with applied brasses. This one is painted in an attractive red-orange.

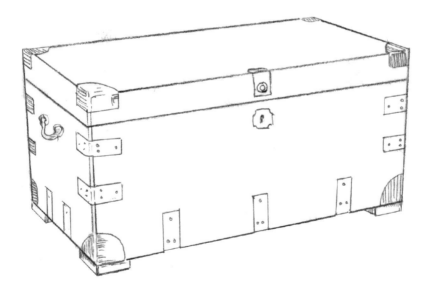

Fig. 1.39 Footies. A small sledge foot is typical on a trunk or sea chest.

The "Harrow" Writing Desk.

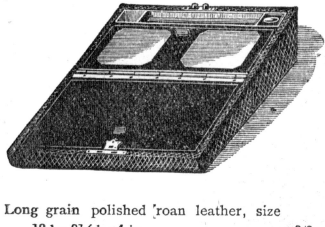

Long grain polished 'roan leather, size
12 by 8¼ by 4 in. 8/9

Do., do., diced Persian leather, size 12 by
8¼ by 4 in. 10/9

Fig. 1.40 A typical writing slope from the Army & Navy Co-operative Society.

The "Winchester" Desk.

Polished roan leather, recess for
papers in slope, fitted complete,
lock and key, 14 in. 22/6

Fig. 1.41 A more complicated and expensive writing slope from the 1907 Army & Navy Co-operative Society.

Writing Slopes

Writing slopes – also called lap desks – were common items among travelers, officers, clerks and anyone else who had lots of daily correspondence. As a result, the line between writing slopes for domestic use and those for campaigning is a blurry one. There might not even be a line at all.

Brass-bound traveling desks were used by many people who never left their neighborhood, much less their continent. The desks were typically made from fancy woods, such as mahogany, and could feature all sorts of flush hardware, including corner guards, pulls and hinges.

Fig. 1.42 A campaign writing slope. Flipping down the hinged section reveals the writing surface and three drawers.

Figs. 1.43 & 1.44 Details. Based on the hardware and construction, this is likely an Anglo-Indian writing slope. When folded up, this slope looks much like a typical campaign trunk.

The construction of these desks has been covered in many other books and magazine articles, so I chose not to build one for this book.

In broad terms, however, the desks unfold in either two or three parts to create a continuous writing surface. The writing surfaces themselves are hinged; you lift those to store stationery and writing supplies. Many writing slopes also had drawers or small compartments designed to hold inkwells and other small items.

Figs. 1.45 & 1.46 Naval chair. This Regency-style chair is circa 1825 and features a mahogany frame and a caned seat. Dimensions: 33-1/4" H x 19-1/2" W x 19" D. (Courtesy of Christopher Clarke Antiques)

Folding Chairs

Portable campaign chairs take many forms, including those that fold up like an accordion, those that simply disassemble and others that fold up using an X-shaped mechanism.

The folding seat might be the oldest form of campaign furniture. The Roman curule, a folding X-shaped backless chair, was quite literally the "seat of power" for that empire. The curule was granted to senior magistrates. It was the throne from which they ruled and the curule traveled with them. There also is evidence of this form being used in China by the military, according to Frances Wood's book "The Silk Road" (2002).

Many of these forms are still with us. Visit any sporting goods store and you will see many chairs that were popular during the campaign era. The only real difference between the old and new is the materials – aluminum and synthetic fabric vs. wood and canvas.

But none of the folding chairs above are suitable for dinner, especially in a naval captain's stateroom. For that reason, furniture makers developed lines of high-style chairs that could be folded flat or disassembled.

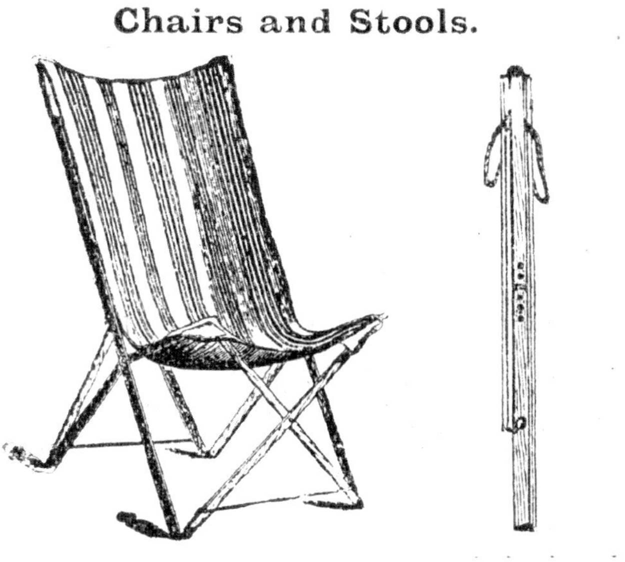

Chairs and Stools.

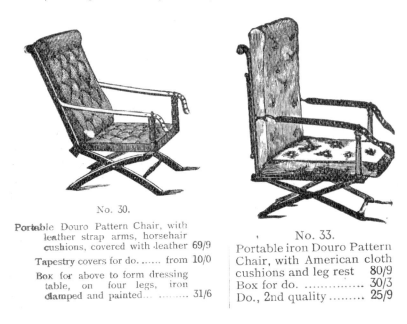

Fig. 1.47 Older than your grandfather. This butterfly-style camp chair has remained virtually unchanged since the 19th century.

No. 30.

Portable Douro Pattern Chair, with leather strap arms, horsehair cushions, covered with leather 69/9

Tapestry covers for do. ...... from 10/0

Box for above to form dressing table, on four legs, iron clamped and painted... .... 31/6

No. 33.

Portable iron Douro Pattern Chair, with American cloth cushions and leg rest 80/9

Box for do. 30/3

Do., 2nd quality 25/9

Figs. 1.48 & 1.49 Portable panache. The Douro pattern chair with leather strap arms and horsehair cushions that are leather-covered. For an additional 31 shillings and 6 pennies you could also get a box for the chair that converted to a small side table. On the right side is an iron Douro.

Figs. 1.50 & 1.51 French campaign chair. This French chair is so clever that I had to include it. The legs fold in diagonally – like an intelligent card table. Then the back folds flat against the seat. Dimensions: 37" H x 21-1/4" W x 18-1/2" D. (Courtesy of Christopher Clarke Antiques)

The classic early form has a seat that folds up (much like a toilet seat). Then the base below folds flat, accordion-style. The chair's side rails collapse, bringing the chair's front rail against the chair's back rail. This form was more typical in the 18th century, but it was used well into the 19th.

Douro Chair

One of the most interesting campaign chairs of the 19th century is the Douro Chair, a very comfortable reclining chair that became a standard catalog item for campaign furniture manufacturers well into the 20th century.

The Douro Chair – named after a river in Spain and Portugal – is a chair with an X-shaped base that folds flat. What makes the chair comfortable is the fact that you are sitting on cushions (covered in leather or cloth), and the back of the chair reclines. The leather arm straps control the amount of recline.

One of the unique aspects of the Douro is that is was available with a painted wooden box that would hold the chair and its cushions. In addition to holding the collapsed chair, the box held four additional turned straight legs. These four legs could be screwed into holes in the box, turning it into a handy side table. So the Douro – and its box – were quite useful for the traveler.

Figs. 1.52 & 1.53 Two Roorkees. Though they use different joinery and turnings, these Roorkee chairs function in the same manner to travel with ease and adapt to any terrain. (Courtesy of the Council of the National Army Museum, London)

Roorkee Chair

While Douro chairs are incredibly comfortable and sturdy, they are also fairly heavy and bulky for a mobile military. As the British military was forced to become more responsive and quick at the end of the Victorian era, traditional and bulky items were traded for furniture that was lightweight and compact.

Someone in the late 19th century invented the Roorkee chair, a Spartan design that was destined to influence generations of modern furniture designers in the 20th century.

The Roorkee, named after an area in India, has no fixed joinery. The legs and stretchers are joined without glue; when the chair is assembled, the seat and strapping hold everything together. Likewise, the back of the chair is but two sticks that are covered in cloth and held to the chair's frame with bolts.

As a result of this shockingly spare design, the chair weighs little – 8 to 10 lbs. is typical. It folds into a small package. And despite all these details, it is remarkably comfortable.

The Roorkee is designed for lounging, not for dining or work at a tall desk. As a result, it is low to the floor, like a Morris chair or any other camp chair. Most Roorkee chairs were covered in rot-proof canvas. Today, reproductions are made in both leather and canvas.

Figs. 1.54 & 1.55 How the back works. The white canvas back of this Roorkee slips over the two uprights and is then buckled at the back. Simple and effective. (Courtesy of the Council of the National Army Museum, London)

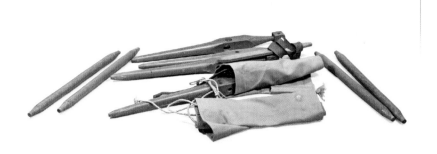

Fig. 1.56 Tapers. Here you can see the tapered tenons on the stretchers that go into tapered mortises. (Courtesy of the Council of the National Army Museum, London)

The leather adds weight and stiffness. The weight is undesirable if you are portaging the chair through the mountains. But the stiffness of the back and seat is a good thing for your comfort.

Roorkees with canvas backs can feel like sitting in a flour sack (I've made several using military-spec canvas). So while leather might not be 100-percent authentic, I do think it is the superior material for this chair. After experimenting with hides of several thicknesses, my favorite is an 8 oz. hide, which is a full 1/8" thick.

If you research this form yourself, you'll find several versions of "improved" Roorkee chairs. These might have an adjustable headrest or sticks that you are supposed to drape your legs over, like a planter's chair. I have yet to build an improved Roorkee.

Roorkee chairs show up in a variety of species, from ash to mahogany to teak. The way the stretchers are inserted into the legs can vary. One common method is a tapered mortise-and-tenon joint. This Windsor-chair joint offers a lot of surface area for the joint without weakening the leg in the way a cylindrical mortise would. Plus, the more weight that is placed on the chair, the tighter the joint becomes.

Some Roorkees are joined with a simple cylindrical mortise-and-tenon joint. Still others have some sort of hybrid joinery – the tenon might be a cylinder but it will have a square shoulder that fits into a shallow square mortise at the top of the cylindrical mortise.

Turnings

As you study the Roorkee chair, you'll also find a variety of turnings used for the legs, everything from a simple taper to strong (but busy) coves and beads.

Figs. 1.57 & 1.58 Squared. This Roorkee has cylindrical tenons that have a square shoulder. This prevents the stretcher from rotating in service. (Courtesy of the Council of the National Army Museum, London)

The classic Roorkee has a turned cylinder near the top of each leg that acts as a convenient handle for lifting an assembled chair. The foot of a Roorkee is typically a straight taper that ends in some sort of shaped foot. Some Roorkees don't have a shaped foot and end in a thin taper.

The Influence of the Design

The Roorkee chair was designed for the military, but its utilitarian core appealed to modern designers. Kaare Klint, one of the founders of the Danish modern style, directly aped the Roorkee chair for his famous "Safari Chair," which was popular through the 1970s.

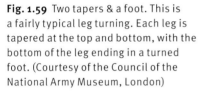

Fig. 1.59 Two tapers & a foot. This is a fairly typical leg turning. Each leg is tapered at the top and bottom, with the bottom of the leg ending in a turned foot. (Courtesy of the Council of the National Army Museum, London)

Fig. 1.60 On tiptoe. These Roorkee chairs always look like a ballerina to me. Without the foot, the chair might have been designed to hold fast in the dirt of a campsite. (Courtesy of the Council of the National Army Museum, London)

The influence of the Roorkee was more far spread than Denmark. Marcel Breuer's "Wassily" chair (1925), Le Corbusier's "Basculant" chair (1928), Wilhelm Bofinger's "Farmer Chair" (1966), Arne Norell's "Sirocco" chair and Vico Magistretti's "Armchair 905" (1964) all owe a tremendous debt to the Roorkee chair.

The influence of the Roorkee for decades after its introduction has always been an important indicator that campaign furniture as a whole might be an underappreciated style. Like the Roorkee, campaign furniture was designed to impress you more with its utility than its fashionableness. Its only real ornament consisted of things that made it stronger. It used woods that resisted the tropics, joinery that didn't rely on glue and brass that held everything together.

In many ways, campaign pieces have more in common with workbenches and tool chests than with delicate dining tables, carved sideboards and veneered highboys. And that is why I think the campaign style is worth reviving among woodworkers.

Fig. 2.1. A camphor laurel tree (*Cinnamomum camphora*) in Australia.

CHAPTER 2
CAMPAIGN WOODS

Here's the truth: With the huge exception of mahogany, I had limited experience working with woods from outside of North America and Europe until starting on this book.

The United States and Canada are blessed with an abundance of beautiful and varied hardwoods and softwoods that are fairly priced and readily available. There really was no reason for me to stray outside my local growing region for raw material or higher inspiration.

When researching this style of furniture, however, it became obvious that woods from the West Indies, India and South America were commonly used for everything from fork handles to cavalry drawers whenever the British Empire went abroad.

So as I planned the projects for this book, I was torn. My gut said I should stick with species that were used for campaign furniture but are not currently endangered. Oak, walnut and (occasionally) birch show up in the furniture record and in catalogs from the period.

But that approach would ignore an important aspect of this furniture. Many of these exotics – mahogany, teak and camphor in particular – were used because they have special properties. Mahogany resists the worm. Teak is incredibly water-repellant. Camphor chests protect objects inside them from moths and other insects. These woods weren't chosen merely because they are pretty or for the status-seeking officer. (In fact, some woodworkers claim that teak and camphor are plain, ugly or plain ugly.)

Plus, I wanted to produce pieces that were representative of the period and the style so I could assess the construction challenges associated with each species. When I build American period pieces, I try to use appropriate stock, joinery, adhesives, hardware and finishes. Why should I skip using the authentic wood with campaign pieces?

My answer to that question was to use old, recycled or plantation-grown woods. Your answer might differ. American black cherry is a good substitute for mahogany. Walnut can look a lot like teak. I don't have any suggestions on a stand-in for camphor. Perhaps you'll come up with something local (Osage orange?) that will suffice.

This brief chapter seeks to introduce you to the woods commonly used in building campaign furniture, though an enormous range of commercial species were employed in some form or fashion. Be aware that there is a lot of bunk out there – there are only three true species of mahogany, yet more than 60 species of wood are sold using that name. So I hope this chapter helps you pick the right wood for the right reason.

The Most Common Campaign Woods

Campaign furniture has been built using a surprising range of woods. While it's easy to fixate on the chests made from crotch mahogany and fine veneers, furniture catalogs of the 19th century offer chests in the common whitewood, which could be spruce, fir, magnolia or tulip poplar.

However, a survey of auction records, furniture collections and museums show that some woods were more common than others. Mahogany of some sort is perhaps the most common species, though some of these so-called mahogany examples might be made out of woods that merely look like mahogany until they are under the microscope.

After mahogany and its doppelgangers, I think it's difficult to rank-order the popularity of the remaining species used in campaign furniture. Oak, walnut, teak, camphor and a wide variety of other tropical species make up the list of woods that British and foreign cabinetmakers used to make furniture. Inside the carcases, you see a lot of ash as a secondary wood, plus oak, pine and various exotics.

I think it's fair to say that campaign furniture could have been built using almost any wood available to the wide reach of the British Empire. If this topic is of interest to you, I cannot recommend any book other than "Woods in British Furniture-Making 1400-1900" by Adam Bowett (Oblong Creative Ltd.), which

Fig. 2.2 "Adolphus Ypey, Vervolg ob de Avbeeldingen der artseny-gewassen met derzelver Nederduitsche en Latynsche beschryvingen," Eersde Deel, 1813.

is an authoritative and groundbreaking work on Britain's relationship to the furniture woods of the world. Thanks to Bowett's research into timber trading records, many of the assumptions and claims in furniture books and auction catalogs have been rendered false or misguided.

And because there is no other species of wood more cloaked in legend and tall tales than mahogany – the most important cabinet wood of the 18th and 19th centuries – let's start there.

The Mahoganies (*Swietenia* spp.)

Three of the hardwood suppliers in Cincinnati, Ohio, carry mahogany, but I have yet to get a straight answer as to where their wood is cut or exactly what species it is. It turns out that this is not a new phenomenon. During the last 300 years, the exact origin of any particular plank has been difficult to determine, and origins are regularly clouded by politics and the particulars of commerce.

There are really only three species of "true" mahogany – trees that have earned the genus "*Swietenia*," a name that was given to the wood in 1760 to honor Baron Gerard Van Swieten, botanist, physician and debunker of vampirism in Leiden.

The most insignificant of the three species (to furniture-making) is *Swietenia humilis*, a mahogany tree that grows on the west coast of Mexico and other Central American countries. The trees are generally small and the wood isn't commonly found in our lumberyards, so there isn't much to say about it.

The second species is *Swietenia mahogani*, which is found in the islands of the West Indies, including Cuba, the Florida Keys, the Bahamas, Jamaica, Hispaniola (Haiti and the Dominican Republic), Puerto Rico and the Leeward Islands chain.

This species is likely the earliest mahogany used by British and American woodworkers, and most of the supply during the early part of the 18th century came from the Bahamas and Jamaica, according to Bowett's research. So-called fabled "Cuban mahogany" wasn't a favored wood until the end of the 18th century and then into the 19th, according to Bowett.

The third species, *Swietenia macrophylla*, is found on the mainland of the Americas and is commonly found in Honduras, Guatemala (and other parts of Central America) and into South America – Columbia, Venezuela, Peru, Bolivia and western Brazil, according to Bowett.

Because of the wide range of this species, it was a mainstay of the furniture trade for many years – and still is.

While amateur furniture makers account for very little of the use of these three *Swietenia* species, the fact is that using a "true" mahogany has a price, both real and ecological, that you should consider.

The truth is that most modern mahogany available in North America isn't the equal of what was available 100 years ago. I've worked with enough modern Honduran mahogany to know that, in general, it lacks the color and density of

Fig. 2.3 Squaring mahogany. Processing *Swietenia macrophylla* logs in Belize about 1936. From "The forests and flora of British Honduras" by Paul C. Standley and Samuel J. Record (1936)

the old stuff I have recycled from pieces of furniture that were dumped at the curb or given to me.

And even if you get your hands on a stash of old stuff, prepare for disappointment. When you read the history of this wood, you will find that it has always varied incredibly in quality. Mahogany that grew quickly in open spaces tends to be lightweight and lacking rich color. Mahogany that grew slowly in rocky or difficult conditions tends to be denser and darker.

Just because the wood is old doesn't mean it's any good. It depends more on the exact location where it grew.

As a result, working with mahogany is an experience that is difficult to quantify. I've worked with batches that were as easy to deal with as Eastern white pine. And I have boards in my shop that seem denser than rock maple and resist every effort to smooth them.

If you are determined to use a *Swietenia* in your work, I recommend being prepared for the worst. Its grain is interlocked, so planing it can be difficult without a sharp iron and a closely set chipbreaker. If you are a machine woodworker, you will find that you have the best luck with a combination of spiral carbide cutterheads and random-orbit sanding.

If you aren't set on using a *Swietenia*, there are other non-*Swietenia* woods out there that will fool most people into thinking they are mahogany, including many African species in the *Khaya* genus. See what's available in your lumberyard. Do your research. Or simply use domestic woods.

TECTONA GRANDIS:—Linn. Blanco.—DC.

Fig. 2.4 From "Flora de Filipinas," circa 1880.

Teak (*Tectona grandis*)

Teak is another wood that is difficult to justify using for making furniture. This species, native to Southeast Asia, is incredibly expensive and difficult to get in widths that are suitable for chests and the like.

The teak I used for this book was cut well before I was born and sat in warehouses and back rooms until it fell into my hands. For me, the dusty and ragged planks I dragged out of storage were an incredible burden – both physical and mental. And they still are.

Because this wood is so expensive, I refuse to throw out or mulch even the smallest chunks. And so I find myself using it on smaller and smaller bits of work – first chests, then tables, chairs, stools and now tool handles.

Historically, teak has been one of the ultimate boatbuilding woods. Its oily nature makes it naturally water-resistant, and its strength makes it ideal for constructing a navy.

According to Bowett, teak wasn't used much in making fine furniture, except for campaign pieces, much of which was built in India and other Asian colonies of Great Britain. During the last couple decades of haunting antique dealers and auctions, however, I stumbled on enough teak chests and trunks with standard British brass fittings to suspect they were built in Britain.

The evidence I have comes from three catalogs I own from the Army & Navy Co-operative Society, which supplied barracks furniture and every other household item imaginable.

The 1885 edition of the catalog states that "The above (furniture) being manufactured at the Society's works, a large reduction (in price) in many articles has been made…." The two later editions of the catalog I own (1907 and 1929-30) state "The greater portion of the above (articles) being manufactured at the Society's own works…."

Of course, the Society had offices in Calcutta, Bombay and elsewhere, so it's possible the teak furniture was made there.

Teak furniture was also made in England by companies such as H. Castle & Sons, Millbank, which used teak salvaged from dismantled ships, according to Sean and Simon Clarke's "The Captain's Kit Bag" catalog (2007). The Castle company used much of the teak to make garden furniture and even furnished the grounds of Buckingham Palace and Wimbledon with recycled teak furniture.

What is clear and interesting is that teak pieces were available to the British, and they were of a middling price – usually less expensive than the same piece in mahogany but slightly more than an oak piece (though in the late 19th century teak was even less expensive than oak). The idea of teak being less expensive than mahogany and about the same price as oak might seem far-fetched, but it has happened more than once.

In the late 20th century, teak was surprisingly cheap and our family bought

No. 8. With middle escritoire, 3 ft. 3
in. long, 1 ft. 7 in. wide, and 3 ft. 7
in. high ; secretary drawer 8¼ in.
deep, 2 small drawers 8¼ in. deep,
1 drawer 7¼ in. deep, 1 drawer 4¾
in. deep, 1 drawer 10½ in. deep.
Teak £10 13 9
Do., mahogany 10 18 3
Do., oak 10 6 6

Fig. 2.5 Available in teak. Teak doesn't show much in the fine-furniture record, but chests made from the tree were available for many decades in the Army & Navy Co-operative Society catalog.

some to make outdoor furniture and planters. That was my first experience with the wood. We didn't use it for fine joinery, so I don't remember much about the experience. But I do remember the smell: Fresh-cut teak smells like barnyard dung. The smell goes away, especially after finishing.

Working with teak is an unusual experience. The boards I purchased were cut more than 50 years ago and were not plantation-grown. They were astonishingly heavy – heavier than white oak.

Despite that weight, the wood machined easily, even with my less-than-industrial machines. However, the teak was hard on the cutting edges of the machines. The teak for a single campaign chest did in a set of planer knives, and accelerated greatly the wear on my carbide table saw blade.

Teak turns surprisingly well and takes fine detail.

However, I didn't have much trouble when it came to working the teak with hand tools. The teak's oily texture makes it easy to saw and chop with a chisel. And it planes remarkably well without much tearing.

It definitely increased the amount of effort required to push the chisels, planes and saws when cutting it, even after applying paraffin to the tools.

On top of this, teak is difficult to glue because of the oil. Wiping the gluing surfaces with acetone right before gluing helps considerably. Using a mechanical joint – such as dovetails or a drawbored mortise-and-tenon joint – helps even more.

Is this wood worth all this effort?

When finished with shellac, new teak looks surprisingly like walnut to the untrained eye. And so some woodworkers will say you have wasted a ton of money on your teak. Oh, and if you have any boatbuilding friends, they likely will resent your using their wood for your little furniture project.

These days, teak is one of the most expensive woods around (about four or five times as expensive as white oak). And it can be difficult to find boards that are wide enough for a campaign chest. When I went looking for teak for this book, I found several boards that were 24" wide and 16' long. Epic stuff.

When faced with a board of this scale, it's easy to see why 19th-century cabinetmakers would use the stuff. However, if I had to glue up a bunch of 3"-wide strips to make a chest, I'd start digging though my pile of walnut.

Camphor (*Cinnamomum* spp.)

Chests and trunks made from camphor show up with some regularity. And though I tried to obtain some of the wood to make a trunk from camphor, I failed.

According to Bowett, there are about 250 species in the *Cinnamomum* genus, which is found mostly in Asia and Australasia. Camphor, or the oil obtained from the wood, has had a wide range of commercial uses, everything from a seasoning in food, to an insect repellent and a rust-inhibitor.

The wood was most likely used to make campaign furniture in order to make it moth-resistant, and it shows up in the Army & Navy Co-operative Society as a liner for storage chests. Later catalogs substitute cedar for camphor.

As I searched for a good supply of camphor, I was told time and again that it was rare, expensive and impossible to get. But while visiting Australia in 2013 I was surprised to find that camphor laurel (*Cinnamomum camphora*), was growing everywhere around Melbourne. In fact, the tree had been introduced from Asia and is categorized as a "noxious weed." Residents were eager to cut down the enormous trees, and many of the woodworkers I met there were unaware of its place in campaign furniture history.

Fig. 2.6 *Quercus robur*, Prof. Otto Wilhelm Thomé, "Flora von Deutschland, Österreich und der Schweiz" (Germany, 1885).

If you can get your hands on camphor, it would be an ideal primary or secondary wood for a trunk or a campaign chest (or a tool chest, come to think of it).

Oak (*Quercus robur* & others)

Oak campaign furniture is fairly common and was – in many cases – more expensive than the same piece built in mahogany or teak. English oak (*Quercus robur*) grows throughout Europe and is prized for its workability and beauty for interior joinery and furniture.

For North American woodworkers, the closest equivalent that is widely available is white oak (*Quercus alba*). White oak is similar in texture, figure and workability to English oak, though the color isn't the same. The *Quercus robur* I've used has more of a brownish cast than the gray color of the American *Quercus alba*.

Still, with the assistance of stain or dye, you can get white oak to fake a pretty good English accent.

Ash (*Fraxinus excelsior*)

Many campaign chests use European ash (*Fraxinus excelsior*) as a secondary wood, particularly for the drawer sides. Sean and Simon Clarke at Christopher Clarke Antiques say that ash is practically ubiquitous as a secondary wood.

Ash also shows up as a common wood for Roorkee chairs, which exploit the wood's fantastic strength and bendability.

To my eye, the European ash is similar in appearance to the North American white ash (*Fraxinus americana*) and would be a good substitute if you cannot get your hands on European ash. However, if you are interested in buying some *Fraxinus americana*, you might want to be quick about it. The emerald ash borer has decimated many ash trees in Canada and the United States. As a result, the price of ash has plummeted. Get it before it's gone.

Walnut (*Juglans regia* & *Juglans nigra*)

Walnut shows up in the furniture record fairly frequently with campaign furniture. Likely the two most common species of walnut used to make campaign objects were *Juglans regia*, a European tree that goes by several names, and *Juglans nigra*, the black walnut of North America.

The two species can be difficult to distinguish, even under a microscope. Historical accounts claim the North American species has a coarser texture, but that it is darker with some occasional purple streaks.

In any case, using either species is appropriate for campaign pieces because England imported most of its walnut from North America and Europe, particularly France and Italy.

Fig. 2.7 *Juglans regia*, Prof. Otto Wilhelm Thomé, "Flora von Deutschland, Österreich und der Schweiz" (Germany, 1885).

If you do choose walnut, you are in good company with other fine furniture makers. Walnut pieces, particularly those that were veneered with figured wood, were some of the most expensive campaign chests in the 19th and early 20th centuries, according to the annual price list of the Army & Navy Co-Operative Society. A campaign secretary in 1907 would cost £13, 8*s*, 6*d*. That exact secretary in veneered walnut would cost £14, 19*s*, 3*d*.

Walnut is one of the most wonderful woods to work, both with machines and hand tools. It glues well and takes a finish – particularly shellac – quite well. And it is reasonably priced compared to mahogany, teak and other tropical woods.

So when faced with all the difficult decisions relating to mahogany and teak – where can I get it? Can I afford it? Is it endangered? Walnut seems the one choice that is logical and historically correct.

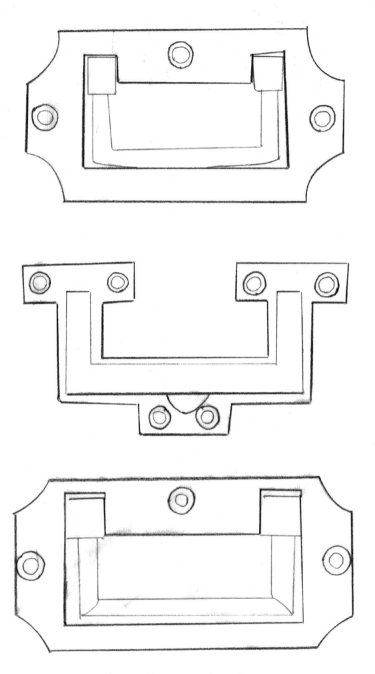

Fig. 3.1. Three campaign pulls.

CHAPTER 3

CAMPAIGN HARDWARE

Few things separate a piece of campaign furniture from ordinary furniture as much as the hardware.

In fact, antique dealers (and the clueless) will pretty much call anything that has brass corner guards a "campaign" piece. You see this especially with writing slopes, a common piece of furniture for a couple centuries that every literate citizen used – not just military officers and colonists.

I consider this a minor mistake and gladly overlook it. After all, most of these writing slopes (which some people call lap desks) were built as tough as a campaign piece, using nice woods, hardware and leather. So they were designed to be taken on "campaign," even if that was just to the park.

What is less forgivable is when an unscrupulous dealer calls screwed-together plywood pieces "campaign furniture" because someone has tacked on some corner guards or rectangular brass pulls. The truth is that the campaign style has had some minor revivals over the years. So you can find "campaign chests" (and end tables, coffee tables and entertainment units) from the 1970s.

So while authentic campaign furniture is something that goes far beyond its hardware, the brasses are a critical part of evaluating a piece. And for a maker, the

brasses are one of the major expenses when building a piece. When you shop for
hardware, it's tempting to buy pulls that look OK from 10', but feel like tin foil
in the hand.

This short chapter is designed to introduce you to the different kinds of hardware and the ways they are made – cast, extruded, bent, welded and die-cast. And
to teach you a bit about the strategies for installing inset pulls, corner guards and
the other inset plates common on campaign pieces.

How Hardware is Made

Like your tools, the brasses for your furniture can be made in many different ways.
The process affects how the hardware looks, feels in the hand and costs.

A lot of campaign brasses I've studied have been cast. There are several ways to
cast metal; the three most common methods for making hardware are sand casting, die-casting and investment casting (and their variants).

While all these casting processes are different in their details, they are the
same in their basic idea: There is a mold made in the shape of the hardware
and it is filled with molten metal. When the metal cools, the casting is finished and assembled.

All three types of casting have advantages and disadvantages for you,
the furniture maker, and I'll be covering them in some detail here. Most
woodworkers are woefully uneducated about the way hardware is made and
as a result make bad decisions. As you are about to see, a little education

Fig. 3.2 Rough behind. One of the sure marks of sand casting is a rough surface finish left from the sand itself. On the backside of a pull, this is not a problem.

about metal casting can go a long way toward improving the quality of your projects. Let's start with sand casting.

Sand Casting

Many handplane bodies (and woodworking machines) are made using sand casting. It allows a maker to produce castings in an economical way. The downside to sand casting furniture hardware is that the surface finish is never nice enough to use as-is. The manufacturer usually needs to finish the visible surfaces and touch points. This can be labor- or time-intensive.

But what is more important for a furniture maker is that the finishing process can make the parts non-interchangeable, especially if the pieces are finished by hand. The upside is that hand-finished hardware with small variations can be beautiful.

Hardware made this way is called "sand cast" because a sand that is moistened with oil or chemicals is used in the casting process. The casting begins with a "pattern," which was traditionally wood, but is now typically aluminum for pieces of hardware. Then either the pattern or a matchplate or some other representation of the finished object is used to make depressions in two boxes of sand – one is called the cope and the other is called the drag. These two bits of sand are put together and the cavity is filled with

Fig. 3.3 Not the same. These two pulls were made by the same maker in the same year and even sold in the same box. But they require completely different recesses. None of the curves (or even the straight lines) match.

Fig. 3.4 You get the idea. The level of detail with sand casting isn't as fine as with some other methods, but it has served well for thousands of years.

molten metal via tubes called "sprues" in casting parlance. Gates are put into the matchplate or simply cut into the sand itself to allow the metal to flow completely through the part and out the other side. This helps the metal completely fill the cavity and helps prevent shrinkage (which is a cause of surface pitting).

After the metal hardens, the sand is removed (and reused) and the resulting metal shape is finished – by grinding, filing, polishing, machining or some combination of these processes. After grinding and/or filing, all cast parts are put into vibratory tumblers filled with a variety of different medias to get the surface finish smooth. The tumbling is the key process that turns a very rough casting into a smooth finished part. Machining typically takes place after tumbling.

Sand casting produces hardware that typically has a substantial feel. Its components are fairly thick. The unfinished faces of the hardware will typically be a bit coarse – like sand. (Proper tumbling eliminates this rough surface.)

These qualities are the nice things about sand-cast objects, but there are some downsides with sand-cast hardware. The level of detail isn't as good as with other casting methods. So a sand-cast lion's face will look a bit "blurrier" than one cast by other methods.

Also, the sand-casting process can result in some variance in dimensions. This is not a big deal at all if you install your hardware piece by piece. But if you want to have one router template for all your inset sand-cast pulls, you might want to closely examine the pulls first and see how close in size they are to one another.

Fig. 3.5 I can read that. Investment casting allows a much higher resolution of detail straight from the mold, such as the manufacturer's name cast onto this pull.

Believe it or not, sand casting (the oldest form of casting, by far) can be done at home or even on the beach. Peter Follansbee once showed me ring pulls that he and other researchers at Plimoth Plantation made on the beach. And Thomas Lie-Nielsen fondly recalls how his father – a boatbuilder – would cast the keels of his boats on the beach.

Investment (Lost Wax) Casting

Investment casting is a more complex process than sand casting, but it is suited for small objects and short runs, and results in some fine details that might not require additional finishing.

The process is complex (and can be more expensive than sand casting), but it starts with a pattern that goes through several stages of production involving creating a wax mold of the object that is then covered in a ceramic material.

Investment-cast pieces of hardware have few downsides, other than the fact that they are typically more expensive than a similar sand-cast object. They allow much finer detail than a sand-cast piece, can have a much thinner cross-section and have the presence of a sand-cast piece.

Orion Henderson, the owner of Horton Brasses, says that investment casting can be pretty economical for very small parts. He says the downside to investment casting is that the metal suffers from greater "shrink" – when the metal cools it

Fig. 3.6 Die-cast. These die-cast pulls are perfectly consistent and inexpensive, but lightweight. One of the advantages of die-casting is that it is easy to cast in threads and other details that might otherwise have to be machined in a sand casting or investment casting.

gets smaller, leaving pitting; the part gets so small that sometimes the part is not usable. The molds need to be oversized to account for this. Because of this shrinkage, Henderson says, investment casting is fine for small parts but not as suitable for big pieces – a bed wrench for tightening bed bolts, for example.

Die-cast Hardware

Die-cast objects get a bad rap. And that's because die-casting has been used with lightweight raw materials to produce lightweight (sometimes featherweight) pieces of furniture hardware. They are inexpensive and look good from across the room. But once you grab the hardware, it can feel insubstantial.

Fig. 3.7 Ejector-pin marks. The small circles are the marks of a die-cast object. Look for them on your Hot Wheels.

Like all casting processes, die-casting has a mold – in this case a two-part metal mold called a die that is machined with hollow areas. Molten metal is injected under pressure to fill the hollow areas in the die. Then the two pieces of the die are mechanically separated and the finished part is ejected.

Die-casting produces parts that require little or no finishing. The parts are remarkably consistent. You can make many of them in a minute, and the individual units are inexpensive as a result. So why do some people dislike the process?

Like all technology, die-casting isn't the problem. It's how it is employed.

You can use copper (or even lead) in die-casting to make a nice and heavy piece of hardware. (In fact, die-casting was invented in the early 19th century to make movable lead type for printing presses.) But in many instances, the manufacturer will use lightweight metals, such as aluminum, tin, zinc or Zamak, an alloy of lightweight metals.

To be honest, these lightweight metals are fine for some pieces of hardware. A drawer knob, for example, can be just fine when it is die-cast. But when you get into pieces of hardware that have movable parts that you grab, such as a drawer pull, the whole thing can feel chintzy.

Fig. 3.8 Or bend it. Bending your corner guards can be easier than casting them. So it's a common practice with this piece of hardware. The big difference is that the corner is radiused instead of sharp.

You can identify die-cast pieces of hardware easily, even if its catalog description doesn't mention the process. The finished casting is pushed out of the die by ejector pins – movable rods inside the die. These pins leave telltale round marks on the hardware. Look for them on the back of the hardware, and you'll start to see them everywhere.

Bent Plate

When it comes to the corner guards that are prevalent in campaign furniture, many modern manufacturers will use thin brass plate that is bent and sometimes welded at the corners.

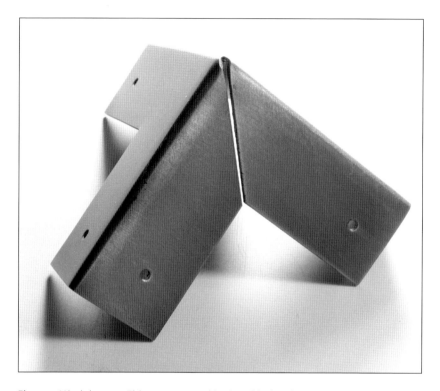

Fig. 3.9 Mind the gap. This corner guard isn't welded at the corner. This makes it easy to manufacture, less expensive and wrong-looking.

This might sound like a cheap shortcut. It indeed is a shortcut compared to cast-brass corner guards, but it can be a good shortcut. The plate is more consistent in thickness than any piece of sand-cast hardware. So installing it is easier because you can use one depth setting on your router plane or electric router.

The downside to using brass plate is that the corners of the hardware – both the inside corners and outside corners – are rounded because of the bending process. The cast corner guards can have sharp inside and outside corners. It's a subtle difference, but it is noticeable once you are sensitive to it.

If you do use hardware made from bent plate (and I do), look for welds at the corners when the hardware covers three surfaces, such as when you have a brass guard designed for the top corners of a chest. A quality guard will be bent then welded. Some of the less expensive guards are simply bent with no weld. This looks just weird and wrong to my eye.

Extruded Hardware

Some of the hardware you'll see in catalogs will indicate it is "extruded." Extruding hardware parts is analogous to making macaroni or using the Fuzzy Pumper

Fig. 3.10 Pretty, standard. Most quality cabinet hinges are extruded these days, though you will still see some that are stamped out then bent. Oh, and there are still blacksmith-made hinges, too.

Barbershop with Play-Doh. Metal (cold or hot) is pushed through a die to make a finished shape that is then cut up to finished lengths.

Many quality hinges are made with extrusion. The leaf and barrel are extruded. Then they are cut to length and machined to accept screws. The only downside to extruded hardware is its price.

Choosing Hardware

So why is all this talk about hardware manufacturing important? I think that hardware can make or break a piece of campaign furniture. A zinc die-cast drawer pull on a teak chest is like a nugget ring on a millionaire's hand.

When I am shopping for hardware for a piece of campaign furniture, I like to purchase a sample pull, hinge or corner guard to inspect the quality before dropping hundreds of dollars on a set for a chest or trunk.

The samples also help me ensure that the color and finish on the hardware will work. And the color of the brass is another can of worms we need to open.

If you buy your hardware from several sources for one piece of furniture, the chance of them matching in color is tiny. And the last thing I want to do after spending $700 on pulls is to open a chemistry set to strip the hardware pieces and color them.

If you like dabbling in solvents and other noxious fumes, you can easily find information on how to strip the lacquer from your hardware and color it with

Fig. 3.11 Too easy. Applied corners and brackets are easy to add, and they might seem appealing after so many hours of slaving over the project. Resist. They look fake or cheap.

ammonia fumes. Me, I have enough volatile organic compounds in my life. I'd rather leave that to other people.

That's why I take one of two strategies when buying hardware: Either I buy all the pieces from one maker to ensure they have a consistent color, or I ask (nicely) if the hardware seller can color the pieces. The better hardware merchants are happy to do this for you. In fact, some will even bring in hardware from other sources and color your entire set so everything looks the same. It might cost a little more to go this route, but the results are worth it.

One last note about buying hardware and I'll shut up: I think slotted screws are really the only kind of screw that looks good on a campaign piece. Phillips screws are a 1930s invention that were intended for assembling cars – not fine furniture.

Once you get your hardware in hand, you can build the piece and install the pulls, knobs and corner guards. There are several strategies for creating the recesses for the hardware, ranging from a chisel and a mallet all the way up to templates for the electric router and pattern-cutting bits.

Installing Hardware

If you haven't installed a lot of flush-fitting hardware, even the simple stuff can look daunting. And the curved, skeletonized stuff might send you back to Shaker knob territory.

I won't lie to you: It's not as easy as screwing a pull to a drawer front and proclaiming victory. In fact, I consider hardware installation on a complicated piece, such as a campaign chest, to be about one-third of the shop time on that project.

And there are tricks that make it easier. I've tried many different techniques for installing brasses – both by hand and power – and can report that it gets easier with time. The best tools for the job: a sharp chisel and a little patience.

When you set out to install your hardware, go over the brasses with a dial caliper if you are considering making templates for your electric router. Before you install the hardware you need to figure out the best way to do it. If all the pulls and corner guards are sized within a few thousandths of an inch, then you can make a router template to install them.

But if your hardware was finished by hand, chances are that you are going to need to install the brass bits one-by-one, each one receiving a unique recess. Otherwise, you will end up with gaps between your hardware and your wood – or hand-fitting some too-tight pieces after routing.

Handwork isn't as slow as it might sound. Making a good router template takes patience and skill. So if I have fewer than 10 identical pieces to install, I'll usually skip making a template and grab a drill and chisel.

No matter which route you choose – hand or power – you need to first determine the shape of the recess and whether it needs to be one depth, two depths or sometimes three.

So take a look at the brass. Basic corner guards are easy. They are simply one depth that has to be cut away for the guard to drop into. The only complication is how to make a router template or how to lay out the shape on the work for some chiseling.

Campaign pulls are much more complex. The pull – either round or U-shaped – is in a deep recess that has to be made first. Then you can make the second shallower recess for the thin plate that surrounds the pull.

So let's start slow. We'll begin by installing a simple L-bracket that wraps around a corner, then we'll move onto one of the more complicated corner guards that adorn the top of a chest. And then we'll deal with the pulls – simple and then frighteningly complex.

Simple L-brackets by Hand

These L-brackets are easy to install once you realize that you cannot simply place the piece of metal on the wood and trace its shape. Because it wraps around a corner, the layout is slightly more complex. But it doesn't hurt to trace the shape

Fig. 3.12 Gauge the width. If the cabinet allows it, gauge in the width of the bracket with a cutting gauge.

Fig. 3.13 Length of the leg. Set the cutting gauge to the outside length of one leg of the bracket. Gauge this on your work.

Fig. 3.14 Chop with care. Cross-grain chops are less risky than chopping parallel to the grain. But you have to do both. Make the parallel chops with care.

of the bracket in pencil. In fact, it can help guide you as you make the rest of your marks. So go ahead and trace it.

Next: Get your cutting gauge and gauge the length of one of the legs of the bracket from the outside of the piece of hardware. Gauging it from the outside will automatically include the thickness of the metal into the setting.

Mark this measurement on the work. Then show the gauge to the other leg of the L-bracket. The measurement should be the same. If it's not, alter the gauge setting and then make that mark on the work.

Now it's a matter of connecting these marks around the corner using a marking knife and a square.

With the layout complete, you can either make a template for your rout-

Fig. 3.15 Clean your bottom. A small router plane is – hands down – the best tool for this job. You can make one from an Allen key and a piece of Lexan if you are a cheapskate.

Fig. 3.16 Relief. You almost always need to relieve the corner of the wood to fit the inside of the hardware. A chisel or a hammer does the job.

er or simply start chiseling out the waste. No matter which approach I plan to take, I usually chop and fit the first piece of hardware by hand. That gives me a feel for how deep the recess will need to be and if the inside corner will need to be relieved or rounded to fit the bracket.

Begin by chopping the outline of the bracket with a 1/2" chisel. Break up the waste by chopping across the grain and then parallel to the grain. A lot of rect-

Fig. 3.17 First gauge. The outside length of one leg of the bracket is the place to start when making a router jig.

angles of waste should jump up from the work. Then you can remove some more with a small router plane.

When you show the bracket to the work, don't be surprised if it won't fit all the way. Many of the brackets are made by bending them around a form, so the inside corner is rounded. Or the inside corner is cast and has some extra material in there.

You can relieve the corner of the wooden recess with a chisel. Or you can tap it with a small hammer (which actually is faster). Then try fitting the piece again. That should improve the fit.

L-brackets with a Router

If you want to make a router template, you'll need some stable plywood or MDF and a pattern-cutting bit with the bearing above the cutter. Because the recess is quite shallow, you'll need to pick a stubby pattern-cutting bit.

Just like when installing these brackets by hand, the work begins by gauging the outside length of the L-bracket with a cutting gauge (or combination square). Transfer that length to your MDF. Then knife in the width of the bracket on your MDF.

Use a table saw (or handsaw or band saw) to remove the waste.

To make the second half of the jig, begin by gauging the length of one leg of the L-bracket and add to that the thickness of your template material. That longer measurement is critical to construction of the template. (If you forget, you'll quickly figure it out).

On the second part of the template, gauge in the width of the bracket. Remove the waste. Then glue the two pieces together so the voids are in alignment. You are done.

Now you simply need to set the depth of cut of your router so that the bit protrudes the correct distance below the jig.

Once you rout out the recess, put the router aside and get your chisel. With the template in place, chisel out the corners of the recess for the bracket.

Fig. 3.18 Clamped on. One bar clamp usually is enough to secure the router jig.

Fig. 3.19 Double-clamped. But when possible, two clamps are better.

Fig. 3.20 Down, then in. Chop the corners using the template as a guide. Then remove that waste with the chisel flat-on. Keep the template in place during this operation. The downward pressure from the template helps prevent you from plunging too far.

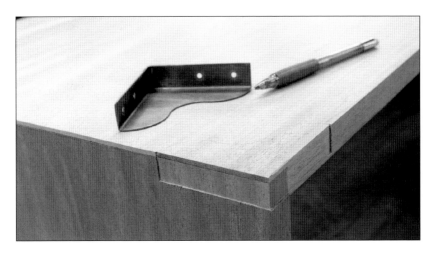

Fig. 3.21 Two legs relieved. When installing the top corners, first cut away the two legs of the hardware. That allows you to get the hardware in place to trace the profile on the carcase.

Fig. 3.22 Whack to fit. After installing hundreds of these bits of brass, I typically beat the corners into submission. But then, I love hammers.

Installing Top Corners

The brass work on the top corners of a campaign piece is only a little more complex to install than a simple L-bracket – even if the corner has a curved profile.

When installing a top corner, it's best to treat it first like a simple L-bracket. Remove the material so the two legs of the top corner fit in your carcase. Use the

Fig. 3.23 With a router. With some shapes, a simple template such as this is all you need to fit the top corner.

Fig. 3.24 Gouges for ogees. When the shape becomes more complex, I usually just clean up the recesses by hand. With some care, a straight chisel and a carving gouge can do the job.

Fig. 3.25 A firm choice. If you have firmer gouges, you'll find this part of the job a lot easier.

strategies outlined earlier – either handwork or an electric router.

Once the legs are relieved, pare away (or hammer) the inside corners of the wood so the top corner will drop into the recesses you just cut. The top of the piece of hardware should now be in its final position so you can trace or knife the shape on the carcase.

Once you trace the shape on the carcase, then it's just a matter of removing the waste. You can do this with a chisel and a router plane, or with a template and an electric router. If you go the electric route, make sure that all of the brass top corners are the exact same shape.

Installing Pulls

When I build a campaign piece, the pulls are the last bits of hardware I install. They look complex, and they are (at times). So it's best to get warmed up on the brackets and top corners before tackling the pulls.

There are three kinds of pulls: the early "skeletonized" pulls, the standard-ish pulls with a rectangular backplate and the Anglo-Indian or China-trade pulls, which come in all sorts of shapes.

I haven't installed enough of the Anglo-Indian pulls to offer any advice. (Perhaps in the next book.)

The easiest pulls to install are the later Victorian pulls that have a rectangular backplate with cove cuts at the corners. So let's start with those.

Like anything in woodworking, it's best to reduce this complex operation into small, simple steps and tackle those one by one. Most of these pulls have two lay-

Fig. 3.26 A hardboard guide. A simple template from hardboard can guide the first stage in installing pulls.

Fig. 3.27 Trace & drill. Remove as much waste as you can with a Forstner bit, if that's the route you choose to go.

ers: There is a shallow backplate and a deeper layer for the pull itself.

Focus all your attention on this deeper layer. If you can get this unseen layer correct then you will have an easy time fitting the rest of the pull.

The deeper layer needs a recess that is deep, long and wide. My first step when installing a pull is to determine the size (and depth) of the recess needed to get that layer sunk into the wood with the backplate resting on the drawer front.

I'll measure the brass shapes on the back of the hardware and try to

Fig. 3.28 Router template. If you are going to make a router template for the deeper recess, make it much like you did for the L-brackets as described earlier. You can piece together a router template from several pieces of plywood or MDF.

Fig. 3.29 Cut & glue. Once you cut a shape for the recess in your template material, you can glue on pieces to make the voids your pull requires.

Fig. 3.30 An added bit. These pulls required a solid area for a screw. So I had to glue in a little bit of material to create an ideal recess for this pull.

sketch out a shape that will allow the pull to drop into the drawer front and still allow the pull's screws to bite into the wood. This simple idea can result in some unusual recesses. Or not.

Once you have figured out a shape, make a template out of some hardboard. It's handy to have if you have a lot of pulls to install.

Put the template on the drawer front and trace around it with a pencil. Then remove the waste with a drill or chisel. If you want to go the router route, then things are a little more complicated.

You can easily create a template for your router by piecing together bits of plywood or MDF until you arrive at a shape into which the pull will drop. I usually make my templates by building up several pieces until there is a perfect hole left in a glued-up panel. But that's how my head works; you can make a template by removing material from a panel as well.

No matter how you make that first, deep recess, that is the hard work. Once it's over you are on easy street. Drop the pull into that recess and trace around the backplate with a pencil or knife. Then remove the waste with a chisel and router plane.

Install Skeletonized Pulls

All of the skeletonized pieces of hardware I've encountered have been sand cast. As a result, I haven't had a lot of success making router templates to dig out the

Fig. 3.31 Trace this. This pull is fitting nicely into its recess and I can now trace around the backplate.

Fig. 3.32 Chisel time. Then it's just a matter of chopping up the waste with a chisel and removing it with a small router plane.

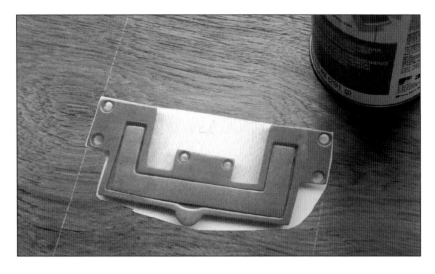

Fig. 3.33 A good scan. Scanning the actual pull and printing it out is a good way to get the exact shape of the pull on the wood.

recesses – even the deep recesses that require less accuracy.

So I have resorted to installing these pulls by using an electric drill to hog out the deep waste, then taking a chisel to the areas that need precision. After studying some original pieces with the hardware removed, I can report that drilling out the waste was a common method in the 19th century, too.

The real difficulty with the skeletonized hardware is that the deep recesses and the shallow recesses are frequently one and the same. In other words, sometimes the wall of a deep recess is what the user sees on the outside of a drawer front. Plus, there are a lot of corners to deal with.

However, I really love the skeletonized hardware. It looks fantastic in the end and is worth all the effort. But you can see why the makers of campaign furniture would eventually reject these pulls – there is no easy way to mechanize their installation.

So where do you begin with these pulls? I struggled with this question a lot as I installed these pulls in sample drawer fronts. Every one of these pulls is different, so making a template is a difficult task. I'm sure you can do it, but I couldn't figure out a way to do it that was faster than the following process.

Take your pulls to a scanner and scan each one at 100 percent. You want an image of the pull that is the exact size of the original. Print out this scan without enlarging it or shrinking it. Then code each of your pulls so they match up with a printout.

Cut out the image and apply some spray adhesive on the back of the printout. Stick it to your drawer front.

Fig. 3.34 Drill the deep parts. Use a Forstner bit and an electric drill to break up most of the waste for the parts that need to go deep. Then square up the corners and fair the walls with a chisel.

Fig. 3.35 Chiseled. Pare as close to the edge as you dare.

Now you can mark out the areas that need a deep drilling – usually the areas that house the pull itself. You are ultimately trying to get the thin areas of the hardware to lie on top of the drawer front so you can trace around them.

Fairing up the walls of this recess is the most critical part of the entire installation process. Some of the walls need to be pared exactly because they will show. So take your time. Press the hardware into the recess but don't force it. The skeleton-

Fig. 3.36 And trace. Once the pull can drop into the recess, you can trace around the thin parts. And you should trace around the hardware. Even though you scanned that piece of hardware, your deep recess might be tilted or shifted.

Fig. 3.37 Final fitting. Don't be afraid to file away bits of brass here and there so that the pull swings sweetly.

Fig. 3.38 Dowel detail. Depending on the pull, you might need to put a dowel behind the pull to push it forward enough to grab it. It is one of the challenges of inset hardware.

ized pulls can be easily bent and that can lock up the pull so it won't move.

Once you can get the pull into the recess, trace around the thin mounting plates. Then remove the pull, chop away the waste with a chisel and pare the depth with a router plane.

And Locks

One last tip on installing hardware: You can use the same techniques above to install hardware such as chest and cabinet locks. The first step is to make the deepest recess and use that to work your way to the shallower recesses.

In the case of a lock, the deepest "recess" is actually a hole for the pin on which the key rotates. Press the lock into the carcase in the place where you want it to go. The pin will dent the wood. Then drill a scant (slightly undersized) hole through the carcase. After that, you will be able to trace around the body of the lock. And once you mortise that away, you'll be able to trace around the lock's mounting plate.

Fig. 4.1. A campaign chest in teak.

CHAPTER 4
CAMPAIGN CHESTS

My favorite form of campaign chest is the one shown here – three long drawers topped by two narrower ones. This five-drawer arrangement is a familiar form that has been with us since at least the 17th century. Yet making this form of chest work for the mobile British Empire required furniture makers to redesign some things to make them more robust, stackable and un-screwable.

In many cases, the most upsetting thing about the redesign is what it does to the way the drawers graduate from the bottom of the chest to the top. With a domesticated five-drawer arrangement we expect the drawers to get smaller as they progress upward.

With campaign chests, those rules can go out the window.

After looking at hundreds of chests, I have concluded that almost any drawer arrangement was acceptable. And after looking at enough of these, I have also found beauty in drawer arrangements that most traditional designers would reject.

Why did designers of campaign chests muck with the drawer graduations? Function. The vast majority of campaign chests were built in two units that could be stacked and unstacked for portability. These individual units were typically similar in size, especially after you unscrewed the feet

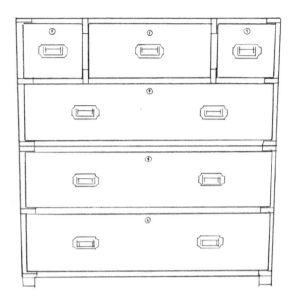

Fig. 4.2 Perhaps a secretary. Many chests like this would house a secretary in the top center drawer. Some would not.

Fig. 4.3 A fat second. The second drawer from the top is bigger than all the others. It might hold a secretary. It might not.

Fig. 4.4 Somewhat standard. In this chest, the drawers graduate from bottom to top like a household chest of drawers. They might not be in a mathematical sequence, but the intent is clear.

Fig. 4.5 Top-heavy. In this chest the top drawers are the tallest. Why? Perhaps there is a secretary in one of the top drawers. Perhaps not.

Fig. 4.6 Ready to go. Even in teak, which is heavy, one person can move an entire chest of drawers around a household.

and placed them in one of the drawers. So the designers had to divide the case into two units. If the chest (minus the feet) was 36" tall, then you would have two units that are 18" tall and would need to scale the drawers to fit those holes.

You can fake a somewhat standard drawer-graduation scheme into that design. But what if you wanted to make one of the drawers a fall-front secretary? The writing surface had to be about 30" from the floor and the drawer had to be about 10" tall. And that's when things get odd. In many cases, such as the campaign secretary shown in this book, the top drawer is actually the tallest drawer in the chest.

Even if the chest isn't going to have a secretary with a gallery, you might want one of the drawers to have a hinged writing surface on the top that is exposed as you pull the second drawer out of the carcase (these are sometimes called "cavalry drawers"). You lift the writing surface to get at writing supplies below. Again, this writing surface needs to be at about 30", but the drawer below it can't be super tall because your knees might not wedge under there.

So the designers would do other things to the drawer arrangement including, gasp, draw the drawers all the same height. In most furniture-design books this is a no-no. This arrangement is often criticized as boring or unsettling to the viewer.

After a rough acclimation period, I quite like this arrangement. It also simplifies construction, especially when cutting out your parts for the drawers. So for this chest I have drawers that are all just less than 8" tall.

Sketch & Pay Up

After you decide on the basic overall height and width, hit the lumberyard to find the right boards for the show surfaces – especially the exterior parts of the case and the drawer fronts.

At the lumberyard, look for the widest board that is long enough (10' to 12') to wrap the grain continuously up the side, along the top and down the other side of the chest. If you can find 18"-wide boards, make the case 18" deep. If you have 16", make the case 16" deep; don't glue a 2"-wide board to the case to make it 18" wide. If you find a board that is wider than 24", genuflect and save that one for a tabletop instead of a chest.

Let the material dictate the depth, and focus on finding one beautiful board for the show surfaces of the case. If you can't find one wide board, look for boards that are 8" wide or wider and glue them edge to edge to make the case sides and top.

Next search out the board for the drawer fronts. The goal is to find one board (12' to 16' long) for all the drawer fronts. Look for something 8" to 10" wide for a regular chest of drawers. And 12" wide if you are making a secretary.

After you get the boards you need for the exterior of the case and the drawers, the rest is easier.

You need solid panels of primary wood for the bottom of the top case, plus the top and bottom of the lower case. These can be glued up from narrower and knotty stock because the only thing that will show is the front edge. Count on needing about 15-18 board feet of primary wood for these parts.

You'll also need some primary and secondary wood for the two web frames that separate the drawers in each case. These web frames are made from pieces that are 2-1/2" to 3" wide. Count on buying 24' linear feet of this kind of material for the web frames.

The backs can be made from secondary or primary wood. Plan on 10 board feet of 4/4 material for the backs.

The drawer parts can also be made from primary or secondary wood. Plan on 35 to 40 board feet for all the interior drawer parts.

Finally, source some wood for the base – whether you are using turned feet, a traditional plinth or simple sledge feet.

Materials to Consider

Campaign chests were made from a variety of materials. The most common woods were mahogany, teak, walnut, camphor and oak. However, almost any cabinet-grade wood will do and a similar example probably can be found in the historical record. I've even seen them made out of pine and tulip poplar.

What is important to note about these chests is that some of them did not have any secondary woods used for the interior pieces. Some examples were made entirely out of mahogany – even the drawer bottoms and backs. This made the chests more resistant to rot and bugs. It also raised the price significantly.

There are lots of examples out there that did use secondary woods for interior components. Common secondary woods were ash, oak and pine.

As far as thicknesses go, the carcase materials should be made out of wood that finishes out at 3/4" thick to 7/8" thick. These thicknesses work well with the available brasses, particularly the corner brackets and straps. The cabinet backs should be made out of 1/2"-thick material. The drawer

๛ CAMPAIGN CHEST ๛

NO.	PART	SIZES (INCHES)		
		T	W	L
Top Carcase				
1	Top	7/8	17	36
2	Sides	7/8	17	17-3/4
1	Bottom	7/8	17	34-1/4
2	Web frame stiles (blades)	7/8	2-1/2	34-3/4
3	Web frame rails	7/8	2-1/2	15-1/2
1	Vertical divider	7/8	3	8-3/16
1	Drawer guide	7/8	2-1/2	13
2	Top drawer fronts	7/8	7-11/16	16-11/16
1	Long drawer front	7/8	7-11/16	34-1/4
1	Back	1/2	17	35-1/4
Lower Carcase				
2	Top & bottom	7/8	17	34-1/4
2	Sides	7/8	17	18
2	Web frame stiles (blades)	7/8	2-1/2	34-3/4
2	Web frame rails	7/8	2-1/2	15-1/2
2	Drawer fronts	7/8	7-11/16	34-1/4
1	Back	1/2	17	35-1/4
Plinth				
4	Sledge feet	7/8	5-1/2	5-1/2
4	Feet	3-1/4 dia.		3-1/4

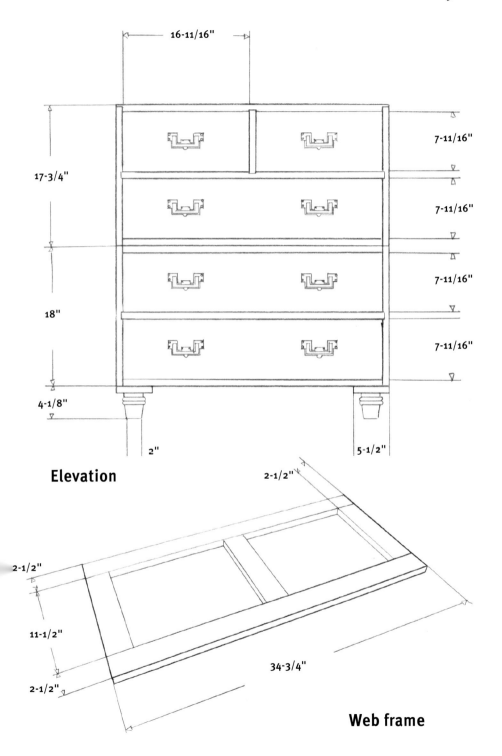

Elevation

16-11/16"

7-11/16"

17-3/4"

7-11/16"

7-11/16"

18"

7-11/16"

4-1/8"

2"

5-1/2"

2-1/2"

2-1/2"

11-1/2"

2-1/2"

34-3/4"

Web frame

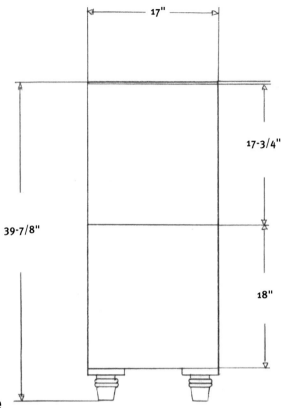

Profile

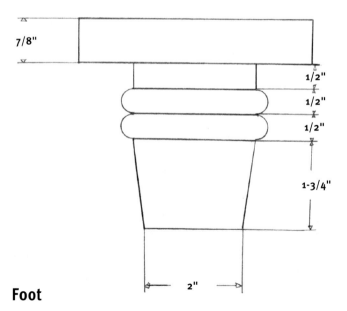

Foot

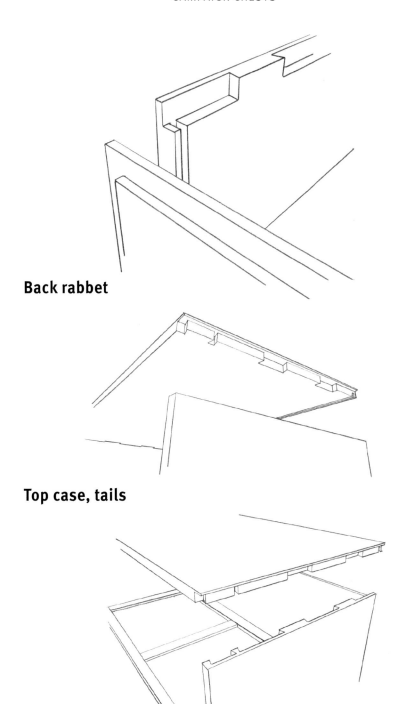

Back rabbet

Top case, tails

Top case, pins

Fig. 4.7 Traversing teak. If you use a jack plane or fore plane with a heavily cambered iron, you can flatten panels with ease. The trick: Work across the grain.

sides, backs and bottoms can be 1/2" or 3/8". The 3/8" stuff is old-school English. If you are going to use turned feet, you'll need some blanks that are about 2-1/2" to 4" in diameter and about 5" long.

Brasses

The most significant investment on one of these chests is in the brass. Buy your brasses before you cut a single stick of wood. As you thickness your stock, you will want to make it match the size of the brass corner brackets. That will make it easier to install the brackets. If your stock is a wee bit thicker than your brasses are tall, then you will quickly find out what a pain in the tuckus that is. A fragile edge of wood is no fun to deal with.

Be sure to order the right screws with your brasses. An 18th- or 19th-century chest with Phillips-head screws looks odd.

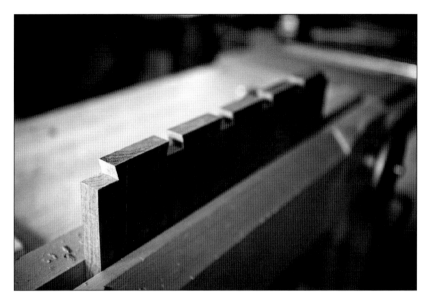

Fig. 4.8 Six tails. When cutting dovetails that are for structural purposes and won't be seen much, use tails and pins that are fairly large. For a campaign chest, lay out five tails or so on the tops and bottoms that join the sides. These tails are 1/2" long.

Stock Prep

When you get into boards that are sized for casework, you have to either buy a $3,000 powered jointer that can handle 16" to 24" of width, or you can buy a $20 jack plane   your choice. Flattening wide boards can be handled by money or muscle. I'm a writer; muscle has always been more affordable.

So I flatten my carcase panels with a jack plane and jointer plane. It's work, but any work on wide and beautiful stock is a joy. So I don't mind the sweat.

After you get the panels to the right thickness, you can rip them to their finished widths. There are lots of ways to determine the right width. The top and sides should be the maximum width your stock will allow – 17" wide in my case. The interior assemblies should be 1/2" narrower to allow the backs to slide into the assembled carcases.

Then crosscut the boards to their final length. Remember: The goal is to wrap the grain pattern around the sides and top of the chest so that the board's figure flows up the chest, across the top and down the other side. This takes planning, but nothing too nuts.

Dovetailing the Corners

There are three kinds of dovetail joints in a typical campaign chest: Full-blind dovetails join the top of the chest to the sides. Half-blind dovetails join the interior

Fig. 4.9 How to see better. Knife lines in dark and porous woods can be murder to see. One solution is to use a fabric-marking pencil, such as the one shown here. The pencil's "lead" is actually a soft ceramic material that comes in bright colors: pink, green and white are typical. All help you to better see your knife lines.

panels of the carcases with the sides. Half-blinds also are used to join the drawer fronts with the drawer sides. Through-dovetails are used to join the drawer backs with the drawer sides.

It is a lot of dovetails. But these dovetails are one of the reasons that so many of these chests have survived. They are (literally) bombproof.

Everyone needs to warm up when dovetailing, so begin by cutting the half-blind dovetails that join the interior carcase panels to the sides. These joints have to be strong, but they don't have to be pretty. The only time anyone will see these joints is when the chest is taken to pieces to move it.

So cut your tails and use them as a template to lay out your pins on the side pieces. When transferring the shape of the tails to the pin boards I use a knife to trace around the tails. Because many campaign chests are built using dark-colored woods, you might have to enhance the lines with chalk or some other method so you can see them.

Saw out the walls of the pins then remove the waste between. You can bang the waste out with a chisel, but because I had so many of these to cut, I set up a drill press with a 1/2"-diameter Forstner bit to hog out the majority of the junk. Then I pared out what was left.

After you get all the half-blind dovetails cut for the carcase, you can cut the

Fig. 4.10 Tidy sockets. Here you can see the points left by a Forstner bit, which I used to bore out most of the waste on the pin board. Don't get too sloppy here. Even though the joint won't show, it does hold the case together.

full-blind dovetails that join the top of the chest to the sides of the top case. This joint isn't hard to execute if you simply take a couple extra steps to make it easier on yourself.

First, harness the power of the rabbet. Cutting a shallow rabbet, about 1/16" deep across the tails, will make the shape of the tails easier to transfer to the pin boards. The rabbet should extend all the way to the baseline of the joint.

After you cut that rabbet, cut a second one on the ends of the top. This 1/8" x 1/2" rabbet forms the lip on the top of the carcase and transforms the joint into a full-blind dovetail. If you are having trouble following the layout, study the photos and it will become clear.

With the rabbets cut, lay out and cut the tails. Take extra care not to nick the lip of the top with your saw – that will show when the joint is together. However, feel free to overcut below the baseline on the inside of the joint. Overcutting the baselines on joints that won't show is a fairly common feature of old furniture, including the campaign chests I've studied. The overcutting makes it easier to remove the waste.

If the overcutting offends a sensibility, skip it. Either way, the only people who will know are you and some future furniture conservator.

After you finish the tail board, transfer the shape to the pin board. Be-

Fig. 4.11 Double rabbets. Here you can see the shallow rabbet cut on the tails of the joint and the deeper rabbet cut on the ends of the top. I am in the middle of chopping out the waste between the tails.

Fig. 4.12 Completed joint. This stack of parts shows what the tail boards and pin boards look like when they are ready for assembly.

Fig. 4.13 For the frame. The 3/4"-wide x 1/4"-deep dado holds the web frame of the carcase. The dado runs through the sides – it is not stopped. A brass corner bracket will hide the joint in the end.

cause of the lip on the top, it can be tough to weasel your knife in there. I use a mechanical pencil then cast raking light across the marks to make them shine so I can see them.

Cut the pins. Nothing unusual here   it's just like cutting the pins for a half-blind joint.

Fit all the corners without glue. Knock the case apart and get ready to cut the dados and grooves for the rest of the guts of the chest.

Dados, Grooves & Guts

Each carcase is divided up by a web frame. These web frames slide into a dado that is plowed into the sides of the case. The width of the dado should match the thickness of the material you have selected for your web frames.

To make it easy on myself, I simply cut the dados to exactly 3/4" wide x 1/4" deep then planed my web frame parts to fit exactly.

When laying out the dados, take extra care. It's easy to forget the lip on the top of the carcase and screw things up royally. In other words, the dado layout for the top case is not the same as for the lower case.

The grooves for the back pieces are plowed in the four case sides and the top. These grooves run through on all the pieces – they are not stopped in any way.

It's now time to assemble the two carcases. There is still some internal joinery

Fig. 4.14 A groove for the back. Plow a 1/4" x 1/4" groove that is 1/4" from the back edge of the case sides and top. You can see how this groove overlaps the dado you just cut. It's no big deal – this is all hidden at the back of the case.

to cut for the vertical dividers between the two top drawers, but it's better to cut those joints after assembly.

I can't over-emphasize how important it is that these cases be square when you glue them up. You can use the back to help pull the case square, but the back can only do so much. When I glue up these cases, here's my procedure.

Prepare the glue. I use liquid hide glue because it sets slowly and is reversible. To make the glue runnier, I drop the bottle into a tub of warm water.

Prepare the joints. If you are building your case using teak or another oily species, wipe down all the joinery surfaces with acetone or lacquer thinner right before assembly. This temporarily removes some oil from the surface and allows the glue to get into the wood.

Apply the glue to the joinery surfaces and knock the case together.

If you don't need clamps to pull things tight, don't use them. If you do need clamps, apply their pads so they press against the joinery only – this helps square the case. Check the case for square both by measuring the diagonals and by using a try square. Check both the front and back of each carcase – it can be twisted. Use clamps diagonally to pull the case square. Check and double check.

As soon as it is square, walk away. Don't move it, touch it or even look at it. Don't be Lot's wife. Let it sit as long as you can – as long as 12 hours – before removing the clamps.

Fig. 4.15 Loose in the rear. Don't glue the rear stile to its tenons. You want that stile to be able to move slightly as the case moves.

The Web Frames

Each carcase is divided horizontally by a web frame. These are mortise-and-tenon frames that slide into the dados. To be honest, the width of the pieces of your web frame aren't critical. Somewhere between 2" and 3" wide is fine. I use offcuts from other boards and just try to squeeze the maximum number of pieces from the material at hand with the minimum waste.

I size all my web frame parts so they fit the assembled case. Then I cut the joinery. The tenons on the rails are 1/4" thick and 2" long – standard stuff. What isn't obvious (to beginners) is how the frames are assembled. The joints at the front are glued and pegged with a 3/8"-diameter dowel in each joint. The joints at the back are left loose – no glue. This allows the back stile to move with the case during the wet and dry seasons. And it helps keep the front stile flush with the front of the case.

Note that the web frame for the top case has an extra rail in the dead middle of the frame. This extra rail is needed because of the two drawers at the top.

Glue up the web frames. Then drive a 3/8"-diameter dowel through the joints at the front stile for added insurance. This is particularly important if you are using teak. It's tough to wipe off the oil in the mortise and easy to make a weak joint.

After the glue is dry, trim the web frames, if necessary, to slide into their dados.

Fig. 4.16 Glued up. Here are the two web frames for the chest: the simple one for the lower case (foreground) and the one with the extra rail for the top case.

Fig. 4.17 For the vertical divider. This is a quick joint to cut by hand. Saw the walls of the dado, rip out the waste with a chisel and flatten the bottom of the dado with a router plane if necessary.

Extra Joinery for the Top Case

You now need to add a vertical divider and a drawer guide in the top case to separate the two drawers at the top. This extra joinery should be cut after the web frame fits perfectly but before you glue the top frame in place.

With the web frame in place, mark off the locations of the dados for the vertical divider; you want to divide the case in half. These dados are the same width as the thickness of your material. They should be 1/4" deep. As to their length, the dado in the web frame should go all the way across the assembled frame. The dado in the underside of the top should stop about 3" in from the front of the case.

When all is well, glue the web frames in place; put glue only on the front third of the dado to help prevent the case side from splitting when it expands and contracts. Add the vertical divider and the drawer guide. Screw those last two pieces in place from the underside of the web frame.

Add the Backs

The backs are 1/2"-thick pine with a rabbet on their edges to allow them to slide into the grooves in the assembled cases. The back should be dead square. And the back should fit snugly, except at the bottom of each carcase. Cut the backs about 1/16" to 1/8" shy of the bottom edge of the carcase to give them some room to expand.

Fig. 4.18 Dado for the runner. Here you can see how the dado in the web frame holds the drawer runner and the vertical divider.

Fig. 4.19 Glued & almost screwed. Glue the web frame, vertical divider and drawer guide in place. Clamp it up.

Fig. 4.20 Screws from below. The No. 8 x 1-1/4" brass screws help support the vertical divider and web frame. They also hold the drawer guide in place.

Slide the backs into their grooves. Nail them to the cases at the bottom edge and to the web frames.

Make the Cases Stack

When your chest is complete and in use, the two units will stack on top of one another until you need to move them. While gravity will keep the top case in place, it's best to have some way to prevent the top case from sliding from side to side.

Traditionally, there were several ways to achieve this, including special hardware that was built into the brass corner guards. Because that hardware isn't made anymore, the next-best solution is to have protruding dowels on one case that drop into matching holes in the other case.

You can use two to four dowels. I used four in the mahogany secretary shown in the accompanying photos. I usually use only two and cannot tell the difference between two and four when the cases are stacked.

First clamp the two cases together so their edges are flush. Then drill a pilot hole – 1/16" is fine – through both cases at each location where you want a dowel. This pilot hole will guide the larger-diameter bits and ensure your holes are lined up.

Separate the two cases. Now drill stopped holes in each case that are the diameter of your dowels. I used 1-1/4" dowels. Each hole is 3/8" deep. Cut the dowels to length – just a hair less than 3/4" long. Glue and screw the dowels into one of

Fig. 4.21 Nails bend. Use 4*d* cut clout nails to attach the back to the carcase. The head of the clout helps keep the back secure. The soft steel of the nail allows the nail to bend during seasonal changes.

Fig. 4.22 A pilot guides you. With the cases clamped together, drill skinny through-holes into both cases. The pilot will guide the lead screw of the other bits.

Fig. 4.24 The dowel. This protruding dowel will slide into a matching hole in the other case, preventing the top case from sliding laterally.

Fig. 4.23 Bigger bits. Drill stopped holes that are the same diameter as your dowels.

the cases. Use the 1/16" pilot hole as the pilot for the countersunk screw. Chamfer the protruding rim of the dowel.

Build the Drawers

You can build the drawers any way you please. Most of the chests I've studied have drawers with through-dovetails at the back and half-blind-dovetails at the front. The drawer bottoms sit in 1/4" x 1/4" grooves in the sides and front. Or you will sometimes find drawer slips glued on the inside of the drawer sides. The slips, which are a type of grooved moulding, then do the job of holding the bottom.

Here are some additional things to consider as you design your drawers.

Every drawer opening is different, so don't just rip all your drawer parts to some number on your cutlist. Fitting your drawers begins with ripping and crosscutting the parts so they fit each opening.

Drawer sides should slide in and out of the carcase just as you want the drawer to slide. The drawer front should fit inside the opening with a slight reveal (about 1/32" is what I like). The drawer back is cut to the same size as the drawer front.

I think the drawer back is one of the most important parts of the drawer. If its joints are misaligned, the drawer will rack. The same could be said of all the joints in the drawer, but the back is a special case because it's easy to get its joints cockeyed. Why? Because many woodworkers cut the back narrower in width to allow the drawer bottom to slide in from the backside and to reduce friction at the top

Fig. 4.25 A fine fit. Size your drawer parts so they slide in and out of their openings. Don't build them oversized then plane them to fit; that will add hours to the process.

Fig. 4.26 Drawer bottom in place. Here you can see how I've ripped the back narrower so the bottom can slide in.

Fig. 4.27 Also narrow at the top. I also rip the drawer back down a bit on its top edge. This prevents the drawer from dragging against the carcase, and it lets air move around.

of the back. I do that, too. But I rip down the back's width after all the joints are cut. So I first cut the back to the same size as the drawer front and plow a groove in it as if it were going to receive the drawer bottom.

Doing this prevents me from making mistakes when cutting the through-dovetails at the back. If the grooves in the sides don't line up with the groove in the back, something is rotten.

After the joints are cut, I rip the back to final size to receive the bottom. And I rip 1/8" off the top edge of the drawer back. This reduces drag and makes the drawer move more easily.

Lots of woodworkers struggle with how to hide the groove for the bottom in their dovetails. My favorite method is from antique English chests I began studying in 1993 with my father. A single straight tail at the bottom takes care of the layout problem nicely. And I like the way it looks.

One last detail: I plane the thickness of my drawer bottom so it doesn't drag on the web frame or carcase below. Planing away 1/16" or so of the thickness will make the drawer move more sweetly. I do this with a jack plane that has a heavily cambered iron, and I work across the grain of the bottom. This gives the drawer bottom the proper texture for a piece from this period.

After the joints for the drawers are cut, glue them up and ensure they are square before walking away. Slide the drawer bottoms in place and nail them to the drawer back with a couple clout nails.

Fig. 4.28 Straight tail. Although this method isn't the most common way to hide the groove for the bottom, it is my favorite method.

If you built the drawers right, they should slide into the carcase with just a little friction. A few shavings here and there should get them moving sweetly and with a consistent gap all around.

The Base & Feet

If a campaign chest has turned feet, odds are that they can be unscrewed from the case and put into a drawer to prepare the chest for travel. This simple little trick greatly complicates what is usually a simple exercise. With most turned feet, here is the procedure:

- Turn the feet with integral tenons.
- Bore holes in the square base blocks on the bottom of the chest.
- Glue the feet in place.

Feel free to follow the above steps if you don't want to go whole-hog on this chest. If you are in a hog mood, follow along with the steps below. It's not hard. It just takes some extra time and tools.

The first thing to do is to cut the base blocks (sometimes called the "sledge feet") to size. Mine are 7/8" x 5-1/2" square. Bore a hole in each that can be threaded by your largest tap. My largest tap requires a 1-3/8"-diameter through-hole. I bored the holes and tapped them. To make sure the threads were vertical, I

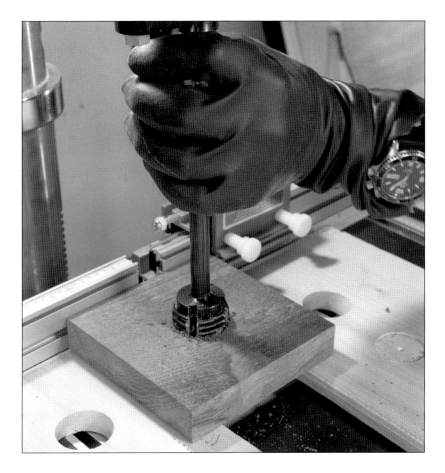

Fig. 4.29 Chuck in hand. Tapping the base blocks is easy with a drill press and rubber gloves. I turned the chuck with my left hand and applied downward pressure on the quill with my right. The trick is a tight grip and a light touch on the quill.

chucked the tap into my drill press and turned it by hand, with the help of some thick rubber gloves. These gave me a better grip on the chuck. It's a good thing I didn't have any visitors that morning. It looked plenty weird.

Once all the base blocks were tapped, I removed all the tool marks then drilled the blocks with clearance holes and countersinks for No. 8 x 1-1/4" brass screws. Make the countersinks deep enough so the screws get some real bite in the carcase.

Installing the base blocks is easy if you clamp them in place while you drill your pilot holes and drive the screws. Clamp one corner down firmly and drill the pilots for the other three holes. Screw those down, remove the clamp and drill the fourth hole.

Fig. 4.30 Simple feet. This foot is easy to turn on a lathe with just a couple tools. The hardest part is finding a piece of teak that is 3-1/8" thick to begin with.

Fig. 4.31 Turned & threaded. The top 7/8" of the tenon is threaded with the thread-box. The rest is turned down to fit into a foot.

With the base blocks installed, you can turn the feet on your lathe. I drew out a profile that I liked based on a whole bunch of chests I've observed. My goal was to keep the feet from looking too much like bun feet or club feet. So they feature two beads with a tapered cone below. Feel free to explore other forms.

After turning the four feet, you need to attach them to the base blocks. The trick is to make a separate tenon for each foot. One end of the tenon has about 7/8" threaded so it will screw into the base blocks. The rest of the tenon can be glued into a hole bored in the foot.

So first bore a deep hole – about 1-3/8" deep and 1-3/8" in diameter in the top of each foot.

Then turn a segment of hardwood so it is the right diameter to be threaded by your threadbox – 1-1/2" in diameter in my case. When you have the turning complete, thread one end of it with your threadbox. About 7/8" or so. Then rechuck the tenon and turn down the unthreaded portion to 1-3/8" so it will fit snug into the mortise in one of the feet.

The rest is easy. Thread the tenon into the base block. Twist a foot onto the tenon and rotate it until it looks good. Mark its position. Paint the inside of its mortise with epoxy and push it onto the tenon. Twisting should get the job done. When the foot looks good, move on to the next one.

When all the feet are positioned and glued, turn the case over on its feet for the glue to dry. This adds downward pressure, which helps the glue to cure.

Fig. 4.32 Ready for fitting & hardware. All you need to do now is get the drawers moving smoothly and add the hardware. Easy! Ha! Yeah, right.

Add the Corner Brackets

Making the recesses for the 20 brass corner brackets isn't difficult; it's just time-consuming and a little fussy. The fussy part is making the template to guide an electric router. The time-consuming part is making the same cut 40 times without making a mistake.

So let's back up for a second. Why cut these recesses with an electric router and not by hand? Answer: There are 40 recesses needed for the corner brackets in this chest. And all these corner brackets were exactly – exactly – the same size. That made them the perfect candidate for template routing. If your brass corner brackets were cast and hand-finished, they likely will have to be installed one-by-one and by hand.

So I cut the recesses for my corner brackets using a 1/2"-diameter pattern-cutting bit in a router. The pattern is made using 1/2"-thick MDF.

If you make the pattern with a little care, you might be able to use it for a few years. The pattern is designed to make only one leg of the recesses for a corner bracket. I fooled around with making a single template that could be used for cutting both legs with one clamping set-up. But it wasn't worth the extra time and hassle. You end up either moving the carcase a lot or operating the router horizontally. I don't recommend it.

So let's make the routing template. Fetch one of the corner brackets and measure its height. Then measure the length of one leg. Make this measurement from the outside of the bracket so that it includes the length of one leg plus the thickness of the other leg.

If this is confusing, see the photo at right.

Make a notch in your MDF that matches the width of your bracket and the outside length of the bracket. Make the notch however you like; I used a table saw.

After you notch out the template, add a fence to it that allows it to be quickly positioned on the carcase. This fence will also need to be notched out so the router bit can go where it needs to go.

Now set up your router so that the bit will cut at the proper depth, which is the thickness of the template plus the thickness of the hardware. Make a test cut or two if you've never done this. Clamp the template to your carcase. Begin making your cuts on the backside of the carcase. Make all the cuts on the back of the carcase to get warmed up before moving on to a part of the carcase that you can see.

Run the router in and out of the template. Turn the tool off and put it aside. Now fetch a chisel and use the template to square up the corners before removing the template.

Once you rout all the recesses in the back of the carcase, flip it over and rout the recesses on the front. These should be easier to line up and cut because the thickness of the horizontal parts of the carcase should match the width of the template.

Fig. 4.33 The real length. Don't measure the bracket from its inside. Measure it only from the outside, as shown here. This measurement represents the size of the notch in the template.

After you knock those out, work on the ends of the carcase. Use the existing recesses to position your template. By this point you should be running on auto-pilot.

After routing the 40 recesses for the 20 corner brackets, you can turn your attention to the four brass corner guards that go on the top of the top carcase. Depending on your hardware, these corner guards might use the same template you just made for the two legs of the brackets.

If that's the case, congratulations. If not, you probably will be better off cutting these recesses entirely by hand.

Fig. 4.34 Begin at the back. Here's the template clamped in place and ready to go. Begin your work on the back of the carcase before you cut the areas that everyone will see forever.

Fig. 4.35 More template work. The MDF template guides both the router and the chisel. Square up the corners of the recess before unclamping the template.

Install the Corner Guards

The brass brackets are a warm-up act for the corner guards. These pieces of hardware stretch out on all three axes on your project. The recess required for them is easy to understand, but it can be tricky to lay out.

Here's how I did it. First, see if you can recycle the template you used for the corner brackets. I was somewhat lucky. The two pieces of hardware were made from brass that was the same thickness, so I could use the same router settings. And the height of the two pieces was about the same.

Unfortunately for me, the other parts of the hardware were different. But their similarities gave me a head start. I used the template for the corner brackets to rout some too-small recesses for the corner guards.

With some of the material routed away, I was able to press the corner guard into place and mark out its final shape on the work.

The next step is really up to you. With other campaign pieces, I simply chiseled out the outlines of the four corner guards and dropped the hardware in place.

But with this piece I decided to make a router template that would remove most of the waste. Why? Because I like the look of these corner guards and plan on using them on future pieces.

So if you see a life ahead of you that involves these brasses, make a template. Otherwise, just remove the waste with a chisel.

Fig. 4.36 First recess. Using the template for the corner brackets, I roughed in a too-small recess for the corner guards. This allowed me to press the guard into the corner and sketch its final shape on the work.

Fig. 4.37 Not necessary. This MDF template is a good idea only if you are going to use this corner guard on future pieces. Otherwise, just chisel out the recess.

One last detail to consider when fitting these brasses: For the most part, these pieces of hardware are made by bending sheets of brass (early ones were cast). The ones made from bent brass look fine – I don't have a quibble with them. But they do change the way you install them.

With the modern brasses, you need to chamfer the sharp corners of the recess. The inside corners of the hardware are rounded, so the corners of the recess need to be rounded as well. It's quick work with a chisel, and it makes the hardware drop into place with much less fuss.

The last difficult pieces of hardware to install are the pulls. For this chest I opted for the most complex pieces of hardware: skeletonized pulls. These brasses are worth the effort. And though they look like a total bear to install, they are straightforward – once you break down the process into bite-sized tasks.

Install the Pulls

For me, installing the pulls was the biggest challenge of the project, not because they had complex shapes, but because each pull was a little different.

So I tried several strategies for installing the pulls on sample boards. To save you some agony, here are some quick notes on each process and the result of three attempts.

Process: Rough out the recesses with a router and an MDF template. Result: Worthless, for the most part. The router bit's bearing or bushing deformed the MDF and made the corners all rounded and such.

Process: Rough out the recesses with a router and templates made from Baltic birch. Result: Better than an MDF template, but the problem is that each pull is different. Do you want to make eight templates for eight pulls?

Process: Scan each pull, print it out and affix it to the drawer front in the place where the brass will go. Use a drill and Forstner bit to rough out the deepest parts of the cavity for each pull. Drive the pull into the cavity with a dead-blow mallet.

With a mechanical pencil, trace around the outer plate of the pull. Remove the pull. Use a chisel and a router plane to sink the mortise for the outer plate. Done. Result: This works beautifully.

Installing the lifts on the sides of the chest components is the easiest part of the whole project. The chest lifts are screwed to the exterior surface of the chest. No mortise or tricky fitting.

The only trick is putting them in the right place. They typically are a little above center on vintage examples.

With all the recesses cut, it is just a matter of attaching all the hardware to the carcase with screws. Then removing all the hardware and preparing the piece for finishing.

Fig. 4.38 Scans. Scan each pull and print out its image. Cut it free from the paper and spray it with adhesive. Stick each in place on the drawer front.

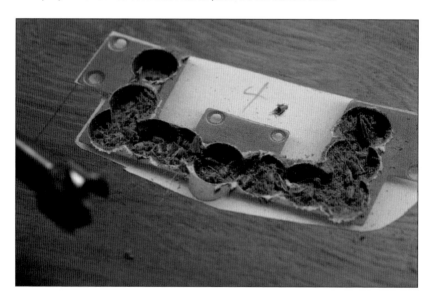

Fig. 4.39 Boring enough. A Forstner bit in a drill can rough out the deepest part of the cavity for the pulls. This cavity is about 5/16" deep. Clean up the perimeter with a chisel and mallet.

Fig. 4.40 Ready to receive. With the deep recess excavated, you are ready to press the pull into position.

Fig. 4.41 Trace & chisel. Trace around the pull intended for that spot. Then remove the pull and excavate the area so the outer plate can be seated flush with the drawer front. The pulls might be warped a tad. Be prepared to slice and screw.

Fig. 4.42 Off-center. Put the lifts slightly above the centerline of each chest compo-
nent. Here you can see how I aligned the bottom of the lift with the top of the corner
brackets. This looks right and works well.

Finish a Carcase (Before Finish)

Getting a carcase ready for finish is a process that begins at the outset of a project
like this. At every point in construction, I try to bring the show surfaces up a
notch. Because the show surfaces could be damaged a bit by working on the piece
(clamping and unclamping templates and the like) you want to get your surfaces
almost ready for finish by the time you are almost ready to finish.

Then you just have to dress the exterior surfaces with a smoothing plane
to bring them to a final luster. If I have done it right, this takes about an
hour for a big carcase.

In other words, you shouldn't be removing coarse machine marks and tear-out
from show surfaces at this late stage.

That's how I work. Other people do it differently and make it work just fine.

The other detail that needs tending is to add the drawer stops. Drawer stops
are little slips of wood that are glued to the inside of the carcase so the drawers stop
when the drawer fronts are flush with the exterior of the carcases.

You can mortise these stops into the carcase. I prefer to add them with hide
glue. The hide glue is reversible so you can remove the stops or reposition them.

To attach them, I first use a marking gauge to measure the thickness of each
drawer front. Then I scribe this measurement onto the web frame or carcase bottom where the drawer rides.

The thickness of the drawer stops is determined by whatever space you have

Fig. 4.43 Stop here. These small drawer stops are affixed with hide glue. They keep the drawer front positioned in the correct place year-round.

between the underside of the drawer bottom and the carcase. I had about 3/32".

I glued in two drawer stops for each drawer. After the glue set, I broke the edges of the case with fine sandpaper and looked – closely! – for any problems.

The Finish Schedule

The teak doesn't need any stain or dye to look good. I applied two coats of garnet shellac and a thin coat of black wax. (You will see this finishing regimen several times in this book.)

When I finished this chest, I was amazed at how contemporary the piece looked before it had 100 years of age on it. Many reproductions look just weird when they are new. This one looked really new. Modern.

Fig. 5.1. A campaign secretary in mahogany (Photo by Al Parrish, courtesy of *Popular Woodworking Magazine*).

CHAPTER 5
CAMPAIGN SECRETARIES

Campaign secretaries were built much like a traditional campaign chest because most of them essentially were a campaign chest where one drawer pulled out to reveal a gallery and writing surface.

The case joinery on a secretary is the same as on a chest. As is most of the hardware, the way the two components stack and the different kinds of bases.

What's different? Two things: the way the drawers are scaled in the piece, and the fact that one drawer was built with a gallery (cubbyholes) and a fold-down or fold-up writing surface.

Because these two types of furniture are so similar, this chapter will focus only on the two major differences – the drawer layout and the gallery – instead of simply repeating all the same carcase-construction steps covered in the previous chapter.

Design a Campaign Secretary

When you sketch up a campaign secretary, the primary consideration is placing the writing surface at the correct height – about 30" – and making the drawer front for the gallery tall enough – about 10" or so.

Because of those two constraints, you don't have as much flexibility in the

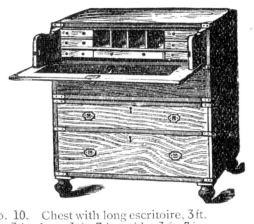

No. 10.   Chest with long escritoire, 3 ft.
   3 in. long, 1 ft. 7 in. wide, 3 ft. 7 in.
   high, escritoire 8 in. deep.   One
   drawer 4½ in. deep, 1 drawer 8 in.
   deep, 1 drawer 10½ in. deep.   Teak £11 10 3
   Do., mahogany 11 10 3
   Do., oak 11 5 0

Fig. 5.2 Standard secretary. Putting the writing surface in the top drawer of the secretary results in a fairly standard drawer layout, as shown here.

No. 3a. Set of drawers, with table escritoire, but without shelves and
   fittings, size 3 ft. 3 in. long, 1 ft. 8
   in. wide, 3 ft. 9 in. high. 2 drawers
   5¾ in. deep, 1 drawer 7 in. deep,
   escritoire 4½ in. deep, 1 drawer
   5¾ in. deep, 1 drawer 10½ in.
   deep. This chest is fitted with
   secret drawer. Teak £12 16 6

Fig. 5.3 Cavalry drawers. With the secretary section in a middle row, the drawer graduations look odd at first. You'll get used to it.

Fig. 5.4 Another option. Some secretaries – particularly those built outside of Great Britain – would have a folding writing surface that worked like that on a writing slope.

design of a campaign secretary. As a result, the top unit of the chest always holds the secretary section. And the secretary section is either a top drawer in that unit or a lower drawer in that unit.

If you choose to make the secretary the top drawer of the case, a standard arrangement, your chest will look like the one shown at the beginning of this chapter. The top drawer will be fairly tall – about 10". But the rest of the drawers will look fairly normal-sized.

Some secretaries had two top drawers; one was a standard dovetailed drawer. The drawer next to it was a narrow secretary. Some secretaries had three top drawers, with the middle one being the secretary.

If, however, you wish to have the second drawer of your carcase be the secretary, things get interesting. These secretaries will usually have the writing surface a little lower than usual, perhaps 26" to 28" (watch those knees). Sometimes the writing surface could be propped up to face the writer. And the lower case plus its plinth will be a little taller than is typical – think 27" or so.

This drawer arrangement usually dictates that the top drawers, the ones above the secretary section, will be fairly small. The first time you see a secretary such as this it looks a bit weird. But you quickly get used to the bigger middle drawer.

Fig. 5.5 Open gallery. The gallery is merely a drawer with a front that folds down to reveal cubbyholes and drawers inside.

No matter where you put the secretary section, it needs to be 7" to 10" tall to give the user enough room to work when the writing surface is folded out. I'd opt for a 7"-tall drawer when designing a secretary where the secretary section is just one of the top two (or three) drawers. For a full-width secretary and gallery, use a 10"-tall drawer, perhaps even a bit more.

About the Gallery

I have examined only a few of these campaign secretaries, so I admit that I don't have an encyclopedic knowledge of how the galleries were built in original campaign pieces. What I am going to describe is the way I saw the galleries built and the way that I built mine. The construction method works well, though I don't promise it's the most common and authentic way.

Think of a gallery in a campaign secretary as merely a drawer with a drawer front that folds down.

Details: The drawer sides are dovetailed to the drawer back using through-dovetails, just like in a fairly standard pre-industrial drawer. The drawer bottom slides into grooves that are plowed into the drawer sides. Again, all standard stuff.

Where things get different is with the drawer front. Instead of dovetailing it to the drawer sides, it is hinged to the drawer bottom with desktop hinges. When the

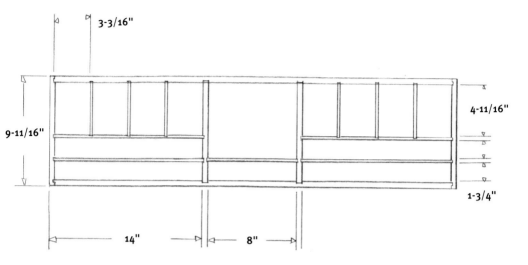

Elevation

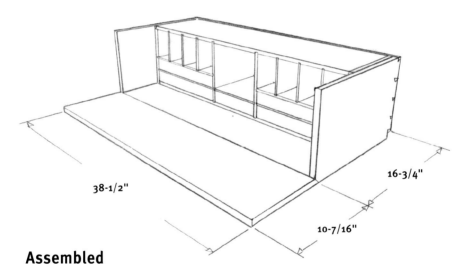

Assembled

drawer front is vertical it attaches to the drawer sides with catches. So when you pull the drawer open, the drawer front pulls the drawer sides along with it. Then, when there is enough room for your hands, you release the catches and the drawer front pivots down; it is held horizontal by brass quadrant stays.

One more important detail is how the drawer front and the drawer bottom mesh with each other. Each piece has a bevel on its long edge. When the drawer front is vertical, the bevel and drawer bottom are hidden. When

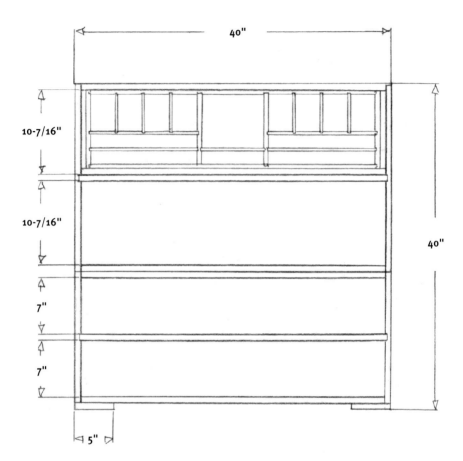

Elevation

~ SAMPLE GALLERY ~

NO.	PART	SIZES (INCHES)		
		T	W	L
2	Top & bottom	1/2	9	36-1/4
2	Ends	1/2	9	9-11/16
4	Horizontal dividers	1/4	9	13-3/4
1	Center horizontal divider	1/4	9	8-1/8
2	Large vertical dividers	1/2	9	8-15/16
6	Small vertical dividers	1/4	9	4-13/16
4	Large drawer fronts	1/2	1-3/4	13-1/2
1	Small drawer front	1/2	1-3/4	8

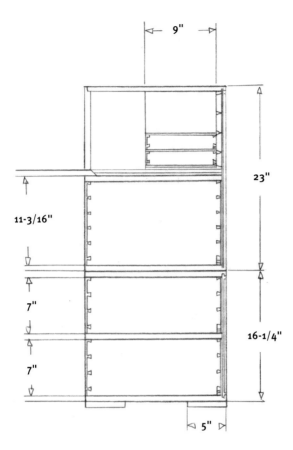

Profile

the drawer front is horizontal, the two bevels intersect to create a flat writing surface. This is easier to explain with a photo than with words. Hence, the accompanying photo on the next page.

So we have a box that slides in and out of the carcase. And it does a special trick: The front folds down so its surface is co-planar with the drawer bottom.

The gallery is merely a separate box that is constructed then slid into the drawer. So now we have a box (the top carcase) that contains a second box (the drawer with the fold-down front). Inside that box is a third box (the gallery). And inside that gallery box are usually several smaller boxes (little drawers to hold office items).

Like almost any woodworking project, it really is simpler than it looks. Once you break the process down into bite-sized steps it's straightforward. Let's begin with building the special drawer.

Fig. 5.6 Critical bevel. A bevel on the desktop and the drawer's bottom allow everything to fold down flat and fold up neatly.

The Secretary Drawer

While this assembly is much like a drawer, it has some notable differences. The drawer sides are 3/4"-thick material to help stiffen up the assembly. You can make the drawer back 3/4" thick as well, though this will add weight.

The drawer bottom is also 3/4"-thick material.

The drawer sides are screwed to the drawer bottom. Because the drawer front isn't attached to the drawer sides by dovetails, you need some way to keep the drawer bottom fixed to the drawer sides and also allow the bottom to move with the seasons. So you drive screws through the sides and into the bottom. Do this near the front of the drawer so that it will push the wood movement to the back of the drawer.

The inside of the drawer is finished. So choose your drawer sides and bottom with more care than usual.

Building the drawer is straightforward. First get all your stock to size so that the individual components slide in and out of the case like you want them to in the final assembly. Plane each drawer side so it slides in and out of the carcase. Plane the drawer back so it is the perfect length to fit into the opening with minimal clearance. And plane the drawer front all around so it fits in the opening with the exact reveal (or gap) you want all around.

Plow grooves in the drawer sides that will receive the drawer bottom. Now

Fig. 5.7 Screw that bottom. This brass screw holds the bottom in place so the bottom will slide in and out with the rest of the secretary drawer.

dovetail the drawer sides to the drawer back using through-dovetails. Don't forget that the drawer back needs to be 3/4" narrower than the drawer sides to allow the bottom to slide into place.

Before you assemble the drawer sides to the back, clean up the inside of the side pieces because these will be finished. Then glue the sides to the back.

Once that glue is dry, measure the opening between the grooves in the sides to determine the final length of your drawer bottom. Cut the bottom to width and length.

Fig. 5.8 Matching bevels. The front edge of the drawer bottom should have a 45° bevel, as should the front corner of each drawer side. After assembling the secretary drawer, you might need to plane these three bevels to match.

Cut a 45° bevel on the front edge of the drawer bottom. The bevel should face the floor, not the sky.

Then clean up the top surface of the drawer bottom; this is a show surface. Then slide the drawer bottom into its grooves. When the point of the bevel lines up with the front of the drawer sides, fasten the bottom in place. Screw the bottom in place by screwing through the drawer sides. Nail the bottom to the back through the underside of the drawer bottom. The nails will bend, allowing wood movement.

With the bottom securely fastened, trim the bevel on the drawer sides to match the bevel on the drawer bottom. I used a flush-cut saw and let it slide on the bevel to cut into the drawer sides.

The Drawer Front

Cut a bevel on the bottom edge of the drawer front. The bevel should face the inside of the case, not the outside. Clean up the inside and outside surfaces of the drawer front then install the desktop hinges that join the drawer bottom with the drawer front.

Make sure the mortises for the hinges are the same depth all around so the drawer front will line up with the top surface of the drawer bottom.

Attach to the drawer front and the drawer sides the catches that keep the

Fig. 5.9 Eye on the barrel. The pivot point is the center of the hinge's barrel, so position the hinge and its mortises so the pivot point is at the point of the bevel.

drawer front locked to the sides. Now you can push the drawer into its opening and see if the drawer fits. Plane the outside of the drawer so it slides smoothly. Then remove the drawer and install the quadrant stays.

Quadrant stays (semi-circular pieces of brass) are no fun to install. Sometimes they are part of an ellipse instead of a circle. Or a parabola. Who knows?

So before I mortise the stays into the drawer front, I screw them to the drawer front in the location where I want them to go. Then I trace the arc they produce onto a piece of paper stuck to the drawer side. If it is a true arc, the arc will remain in the path as I move the drawer front up and down. If it is not a true arc, trace the arc of the quadrant stays in four or five different positions.

This will give you an indication of the true path of the stays across the drawer side. And then you will be able to see what sort of channel you need to cut to allow the stays to travel without binding.

I remove the paper from the drawer side and use that to make two router templates – one for the bottom arc, a second for the top arc. Then I rout the channel using those templates.

With that nasty bit of business taken care of, I can then mortise the stays into the drawer front and also mortise the keeper into the drawer sides. The keeper keeps the stay from wandering.

This is a good time to mortise the pulls into the drawer front. Then get the thin wood ready for the gallery.

Figs. 5.10 & 5.11 Touchy security. You need quadrant stays to prevent the drop-front from over-extending itself and ripping out your desktop hinges. Careful layout and patterns ensure they will move smoothly through the drawer side. Note that on some secretaries, the drawer side was veneered after the quadrant stays were installed.

Fig. 5.12 Fit before nailing. The sides, top and bottom of the gallery all fit into the top drawer. Confirm their fit before putting the gallery together with glue and nails.

Build the Gallery

While people ooh and ahh over the galleries in secretaries, galleries usually are the easiest piece of woodworking in the entire project. Galleries don't require a lot of structural strength; they just have to hold envelopes, paperclips and (gasp) rubber bands.

So if you've never built one, don't worry.

Most galleries are joined with dados, glue and nails. Still others are joined with V-grooves. Almost any joinery method will do, so the real challenge is the layout – getting the cubbyholes, dividers and drawers spaced equally apart.

So as long as you don't get your parts mixed up, you should be able to cut the dados and rabbets you need without too much hassle. The rest of the job is just glue, clamps and nails.

The gallery doesn't have a back; it doesn't need one because the back of the drawer acts as a back to the gallery. So once you nail the gallery frame together you are basically done. The only thing left to do is to fasten the gallery into the drawer.

While you can nail and glue the gallery in place, I prefer to use a couple screws so that I can remove the gallery for finishing. Oftentimes the gallery is finished differently than the exterior carcase. In fact, you will find it common to have the secretary part of a chest trimmed out in satinwood to contrast with the primary wood – teak, mahogany, walnut or oak.

Many galleries have drawers and secret compartments. While I'll leave the secret compartments to other writers, the drawers are fairly standard period English drawers. The drawer sides join the back with through-dovetails. The sides join the drawer front with half-blinds. The bottom can be slid into the drawer box via grooves. Or the bottom can be rabbeted and nailed into the sides and front. The drawers don't ever have to hold much weight, so this approach works well.

The desktop can be covered in baize, leather or left as finished wood. And you can decorate a gallery using period details appropriate to pieces from the 1740s up through the Victorian era, so it's difficult to say what was typical with campaign pieces or what you should do.

My recommendation when building a campaign secretary would be to study pieces from the British furniture era you are most interested in. Take some ideas from high-style pieces and tone them down a bit for your campaign piece. It's not hard; campaign pieces are already understated echoes of high-style pieces.

Installing the Secretary Section

For me, the tricky part about installing a drawer that is also a secretary is getting the drawer to move when you want it to move and to stop moving when you want to work on the writing surface.

Part of the trick is, of course, maintaining a tight fit between the drawer and carcase. But that's not enough. When you drop the writing surface and it is cantilevered out 10" from the front of the chest, a little wiggle is quite distracting.

You can tighten things up by using some ultra-high molecular weight tape, sometimes called "drawer tape," which can tighten up the fit between the carcase and the secretary without adding much friction.

When you've taken that as far as it can go, the next step is to add wedges to the carcase that will prevent you from pulling the secretary out of the carcase accidentally and will lock the secretary section in place when pulled fully forward into the "working" position.

The trick to this trick is to make some thin wooden wedges and nail them to the underside of the top of the carcase. The thin section of the wedge should point to the rear of the carcase. And the wedge should restrain the secretary from moving past a certain point where the guts of the secretary (such as the top of the gallery) are revealed.

You find the sweet spot for these wedges via trial and error. Place the wedges between the gallery and underside of the top in the exact spot where you want the writing surface to be. Trim the wedges in length if necessary. Fasten them in place with nails only. You want to be able to pry the wedges off the carcase so that you can repair the secretary if necessary.

This simple trick saves a lot of time over fastening some kind of blind chain between the back of the secretary and the carcase. Two wedges are much simpler

to install. The wedges I used had a 7° angle from the tip – not because that is historically correct, but because it is an angle that has worked on wedging chair joints so
many times before.

Finishing Up

With this secretary, I opted to finish the gallery with garnet shellac only. The
exterior of the case was colored with a brown pigment stain and shellac. The
contrast between the interior and exterior draws the eye to the cubbyholes and
drawers inside.

This piece is now in the possession of my father. He's a U.S. Army veteran of
the Vietnam War, and I couldn't think of anyone else who could get more use from
the secretary. Even after all these years and technological advances, my father is
still a man who settles things via handwritten letters.

Fig. 6.1. A camp stool in teak with latigo
bridle leather and copper rivets.

Marching Soldier

CHAPTER 6
FOLDING CAMP STOOL

T hree-legged folding stools appear in many Western cultures, including the French, English and American. They have been popular with soldiers, sportsmen, campers and artists for at least two centuries.

This stool is a great introductory project to campaign furniture, especially if you are new to turning or working with leather. There are only three pieces of wood, four pieces of leather and some metal hardware. You can easily build one in a day.

Choosing Materials

I have seen some of these camp stools built using dowels, and they are strong enough to hold most people. However, I like to build them from mahogany, teak or ash that has dead-straight grain. I've had nightmares about getting a stick stuck in my backside from a stool disaster.

If you can build the stool with riven stock (oak or ash are good choices), it will be quite strong. Many original stools used 1"-diameter legs. However, my recommendation is to use stouter stock. I have built reproductions with 1"-diameter legs, and they felt too springy under my 185-pound frame.

You don't need to make the legs baseball bats, but try for something between

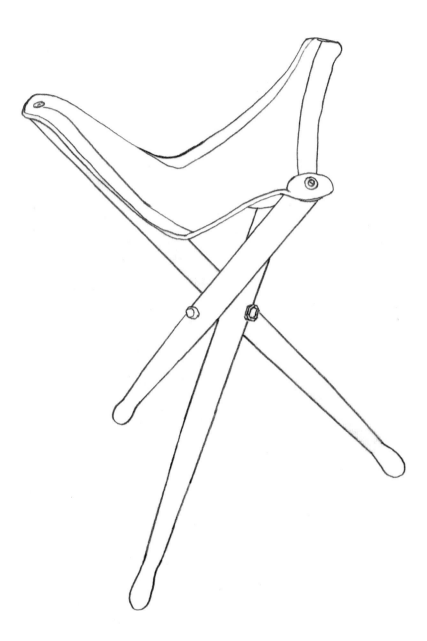

Fig. 6.2 Have a seat. While some of these stools show up with four legs, the three-legged ones are easier to build and are better on rough terrain. This is a drawing of an ash version from the 19th century with a stitched leather seat.

1-1/8" diameter to 1-1/4" diameter. The leather can be almost anything 7 ounces (just shy of 1/8" thick) or heavier. Vegetable-tanned leather that you dye yourself is a particularly strong choice.

You also will need rivets to join the leather pieces – unless you are skilled at hand-stitching. While hollow rivets (sometimes called rapid rivets) are inexpensive, easy to find and strong enough, I prefer the look and unerring permanence of solid copper rivets. I used No. 9 rivets with posts that are 1/2" long.

To attach the leather to the wooden legs, you'll need three No. 10 x 1-1/2"-long brass screws plus matching finishing washers.

Finally, you'll need the hardware that allows the legs to open and shut. Traditionally, this was a three-headed bolt that once was easy to find. Now, that hardware is rare in North America. If you are a blacksmith or have access to a good welder, making a three-way bolt is straightforward. I have seen a couple of these bolts for sale in England, but the price with shipping to the United States was more than the cost of the bolt itself.

So I looked for a different way. Luckily, the Internet is good for something other than photos of cats playing keyboards. One maker of custom stools uses some off-the-rack hardware to make an effective three-way bolt and shares that information freely on his web site.

Here's what you need for legs that are up to 1-1/4" in diameter:

- A hex-headed bolt with a 5/16" shank that is long enough to pass through two of the legs and protrude out the other side by 1/2". A 3"-long hex-head bolt will work with 1-3/16"-diameter legs.
- An eyebolt with a 1/4" or 5/16" shank that is long enough to pass through one of the legs and protrude out the other side by 1/4". (Note: You can hacksaw any of this threaded hardware to length. An eyebolt that has a total length of 2-1/2" should be sufficient.)
- Two acorn-headed nuts.
- Three washers.
- 15 No. 9 copper rivets.

Turn the Legs

The three legs are easy to turn, even if your favorite turning tool is #80-grit sandpaper. Turn the legs to round using a roughing gouge or carbide-tipped roughing tool. Create a smooth, clean cylinder of about 1-1/4" in diameter with a skew or other finishing tool.

The feet shown are 1-3/16" in diameter and 5/8" tall. Make the feet by turning down the foot. Then turn the ankle to 7/8" in diameter. Round the foot, then taper the rest of the leg down to the ankle. The taper should begin 6" from the bottom of the leg.

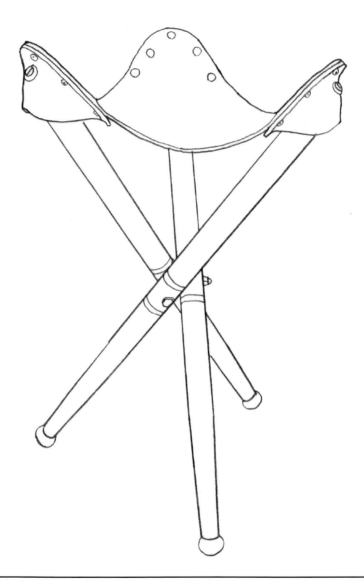

❧ Folding Camp Stool ❧

NO.	PART	SIZES (INCHES)		
		T	W	L
3	Legs	1-1/4 dia.		23-3/4
1	Seat	7 oz.	13-1/2	13-1/2
3	Lips	7 oz.	3	8

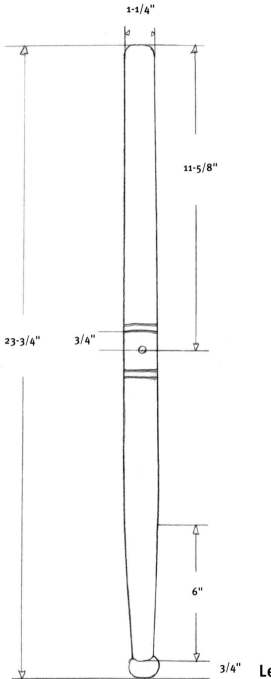

1-1/4"

11-5/8"

23-3/4"

3/4"

6"

3/4"

Leg Elevation

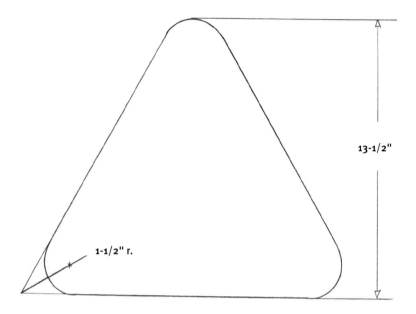

13-1/2"

1-1/2" r.

Seat Plan

Scale: |← 1" →|

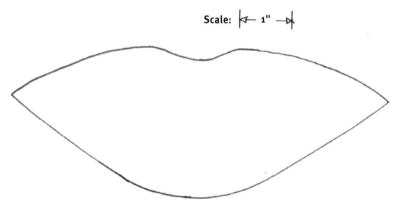

Lips Plan

I added four small grooves where the hardware holes will go – two above the hardware and two below. Little details such as these grooves and beads make the legs look like something fancier than three store-bought dowels.

Sand the legs to remove any rough tool marks. I finished the legs on the lathe. First I burnished the surface with a "polissoir" (a French polishing tool made from tightly bound broom corn). Then I applied beeswax to the legs with the workpiece spinning. I used the polissoir to drive the beeswax into the pores of the wood (again, while the lathe was spinning). Then I used a rough cotton cloth (I'd like to

Fig. 6.3 A bulbous foot. The foot can be almost any shape, from a bead similar to the foot of the Roorkee to this teardrop.

Fig. 6.4 Not original. These little grooves add some visual interest to the joint. However, they're not a detail I found on any original stool. So skip them if you are going for authenticity.

Figs. 6.5 & 6.6 Dead center. The holes for the hardware need to be bored through the middle so the leg isn't weak. A cradle helps hold the legs for drilling, no matter how you make the hole. Drill the hole so the brad point of the bit barely pokes through the leg (right). Rotate the leg so the tiny hole left from the brad point is facing up. Finish the hole.

be fancy and say it was muslin, but it was an old bag that held corn grits) to buff the wax. Then I applied another coat of wax and buffed that.

If you want to add a little age to the wood, apply a coat of black wax and push it into the grooves and pores. Let the wax set up then buff it.

Wax is not a permanent finish, but it is easily renewed or repaired if your stool is for the drawing room instead of the campsite.

Figs. 6.7 & 6.8 Common hardware. The bolt, eyebolt, washers and nuts are all items found easily at a half-decent hardware store.

Bore Three Holes

All three holes are located in the same spot on each of the three legs and should be the same diameter – just big enough to allow the hardware to pass through. The holes are located 11-5/8" down from the top of the legs.

The best way to bore these holes is with a drill press or hand-powered post drill. You want the hole to be dead straight and pass through the middle of the leg. If you are a whiz with a hand drill or cordless drill then go for it.

Install the Hardware

Strip the hardware of its zinc if you like – I use a citric acid solution for this. Here's how the hardware goes together:

- Put a washer on the bolt. Push the bolt through one leg.
- Place the eyebolt on the post of the bolt. Put the other leg on the bolt.
- Add a washer to the end of the bolt, then drive on the acorn nut.
- Push the post of the eyebolt through the third leg. Add a washer and acorn nut.

Drill pilot holes that are deep enough to receive the No. 10 screws into the top ends of the legs.

Leather Seat

The seat is four pieces of material: a triangular seat and three pockets that look a bit like lips when you cut them out. When I cut out leather, I make patterns for my pieces from thin MDF or hardboard – usually 1/4"-thick material.

Put the patterns on the leather and cut out the seat and three lips using a sharp utility knife.

You can hand-stitch the lips to the seat. If you aren't up for stitching, rivets work well and give the project a military flair.

Secure each lip to the seat first with one rivet at one of the tips of the seat. Punch a snug hole for the rivet through both pieces of leather, drive on the washer or "burr," snip off the excess and peen the post over the burr.

Now bend one end of the lip up and rivet the end to the seat about 1/4" from the end of the lip. Repeat for the other end of the lip. Finally, add two more rivets between the three existing rivets. Repeat the whole process for the other two corners.

One quick note on neatness: Be sure to put the burr so it faces the floor for all these joints.

After the pockets are riveted, use a sharp utility knife to trim any little bits of the pocket that aren't flush to the seat.

If you purchased undyed leather, finish the leather with a dye, oil and

Fig. 6.9 Knife work. You will probably make more than one stool, so make plywood patterns of the seat parts and cut them out using a sharp utility knife.

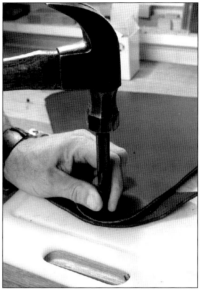

Fig. 6.10 First punch. Using a leather punch, make a hole through the seat and pocket piece. I'm using a kitchen cutting board as a backer.

Fig. 6.11 Insert the rivet. Put the rivet through the holes. The flat face of the rivet should be on the top surface of the seat.

Fig. 6.12 Like a washer. The "burr" part of a traditional rivet is what pinches the leather. Place it over the post. Then drive it on the post with a rivet setter.

Fig. 6.13 Snip it. The post of the rivet should extend about 1/16" or so from the burr. I use nail pincers to snip the post to length.

Fig. 6.14 Peened. Some people peen the rivet freehand with a hammer. I use a rivet setter, which makes a tidy dome. It's personal preference.

Fig. 6.15 Five rivets. Each pocket is secured with five rivets. One at the peak of the curve. Rivet the ends of the lips, then fill in with the rivets between.

When Reproductions Fail

When I build a reproduction, I am loathe to make a significant change to its design until I've built one as close to the original as possible.

It's easy for the modern mind to feel superior to a dead brain. And often we make changes that are unnecessary or reduce the functionality of the original.

When I built my first campaign stool, I stuck to an original pattern that used 1"-diameter legs. They looked spindly, but I didn't condemn them until I had sat on an exact repro. So I turned up six 1"-diameter legs for two mahogany stools. The grain was dead-straight.

I assembled the first stool, put it on the shop floor and sat down as gently as I could. As soon as my weight shifted from my feet to my butt I heard a snap. I stood up with visions of a trip to the emergency room for a stick-ectomy.

One of the three legs had snapped where the hardware penetrated the leg.

Despite this failure, I assembled the second stool with the remaining 1"-diameter legs and tested it. Those legs held together fine, which led me to think that perhaps the one broken leg was a piece of brash wood.

But I didn't like the feel of the stool with 1"-diameter legs. It was too springy. So I went back to the lathe and turned legs of varying diameters, from a shade more than 1" to 1-1/4". After assembling these stools and asking people to sit on them, I found that 1-1/4" was the diameter I liked best. I'm 185 pounds, and people heavier than me (up to 250 pounds) felt comfortable on the stool.

If you don't believe me, the good news is that this stool uses little wood and can be knocked out quickly. Give it a try yourself. But if you opt for skinny legs, make sure your health insurance is paid up.

Fig. 6.16 Finishing washers. The brass washer gives the screw head some extra bite into the leather – and it looks nice, too.

wax. Burnish the edges with a piece of wood and a little spit (water will do nicely as well).

Attach the seat to the legs. Punch a clearance hole through each lip that will allow a No. 10 screw to pass. Screw the leather to the legs with a finishing washer under the head of each screw.

That's all there is to it. You can make the stool easy to transport by making a belt that will go around the girth of the closed stool and screwing that belt to one leg. Or you could make a canvas bag embroidered with your football team's logo. After all, when going into battle, it's always best to fly your colors.

Make a 3-way Bolt

As I was finishing work on this book, woodworker Mike Siemsen sent me a clever three-way bolt he had made from off-the-rack hardware. According to Siemsen, here's how to make it. Hardware needed:

- A 1/2"-13 heavy hex nut. (Regular nuts will not work well; get low carbon, not hardened.)
- Three 5/16"-18 x 2-1/4" bolts (machine screws, get low carbon, not hardened.)
- One 5/16"-18 nut (for cutting off the bolts to length).
- Three 5/16" washers.

You will also need a 5/16"-18 tap, a drill for the pilot hole (F-size bit which is .257"; 1/4" will probably work) and a drill press.

Center punch the center of every other face on the 1/2" heavy hex nut, put it in a drill press vise and bore the pilot holes for the tap. You can then either run the tap by hand or put the tap in the drill press and turn it by hand, no power! Keep things square to the face being drilled.

Next take the three 5/16" bolts, screw the nut on them all the way up to the unthreaded portion and saw off the excess end. Remove the nut and file or grind the burr off. It is important that the unthreaded portion be around 1-1/4" long.

You can blacken the hardware, or remove the hardware's zinc coating using a citric acid solution and let it patinate naturally. The hole in the 1/2" nut is a nice place to add a wooden cap or a small turned finial.

Fig. 7.1. A Roorkee chair in sapele with oiled latigo seat covers.

Sword Supported

CHAPTER 7

ROORKEE CHAIRS

The lightweight and incredibly portable Roorkee chair was a mainstay of the British military up until World War II.

The portable chair also was a popular item for campers, adventurers and those on safari and was featured in the catalogs of Maple & Co., London, and The Army & Navy Co-operative Society, Limited, which was an immense tome of household and warmonger essentials in colonial-era Britain.

Named after the British headquarters of the Indian Army Corps of Engineers in northern India, this portable chair was developed in the final years of the 19th century as the British military become more mobile after humiliations it suffered in South Africa during the second Boer War (1899-1902).

Compared to other British camp chairs of its day – and don't even get me started on what the French were sitting in – the Roorkee (sometimes spelled "Roorkhee" in earlier sources) is a triumph of engineering and materials. It weighs less than 13 pounds. It breaks down quickly (about five minutes if you know what you are doing). It takes up little space when disassembled (8" x 8" x 24"). And it is shockingly comfortable to sit in no matter where you place it. Because it has no fixed joinery, the legs and stretchers move to accommodate uneven terrain and (almost) any sitter. (More on that "almost" in a few moments.)

While all that history is quite interesting, what is more fascinating is how the war-a-day Roorkee chair directly influenced generations of modern furniture designers. Marcel Breuer's "Wassily" chair (1925), Le Corbusier's "Basculant" chair (1928), Wilhelm Bofinger's "Farmer Chair" (1966) and Vico Magistretti's "Armchair 905" (1964) all owe a tremendous debt to the Roorkee chair.

The chair wasn't just the missing link between the Victorians and 20th-century *avant-garde* designers. It also made it into many homes in Europe and America as the "Safari Chair" produced by Kaare Klint, the father of modern Danish furniture design.

The Safari Chair and its imitators were so ubiquitous that many people don't even recognize them as related to the Roorkee or as anything other than mid-century modern room clutter.

I've made more than a dozen of these chairs and have explored many of their different forms. I love the chair – it's something you can almost fall asleep in. But you do need to keep a sharp eye on the joinery and the scale of the chair's components. Unlike a Morris chair, for example, the Roorkee chair is definitely not over-built. In fact, the chair is designed to stretch its materials to their limits.

And because Americans occupy more airspace than a typical 19th-century British officer, you need to be careful. Otherwise you will look like a fool, like I did in 2012.

Design a Roorkee

I gave my first presentation on campaign-style furniture at the Woodworking in America conference in Pasadena, Calif., in 2012. As part of the presentation, I brought one of the Roorkee chairs I'd made from my first batch. This was a chair that followed the earliest dimensions that I could find. Let's call it the "1898 chair."

The chair was made using mahogany, a brown leather called "Crazy Horse" and mahogany dowels I'd purchased from a reputable manufacturer.

During my presentation, I invited members of the audience to sit in the chair. They did. More than 20 people plopped into the chair, wiggled their butts around and got a feel for the chair.

They liked the way it sat. That was no surprise. When made from a stout leather, the chair holds you in all the right places.

But after two days of people sitting in the chair, the leather began to stretch. A lot.

The leather arms sagged and swung like a worn-out udder. The back held up fine. But the seat stretched and sat a couple inches (inches!) lower than when I'd built it.

I fixed the seat by tightening the buckles. Yay buckles. And I punched new holes in the arms to pull them tight.

During the last presentation, one of the audience members sat in the

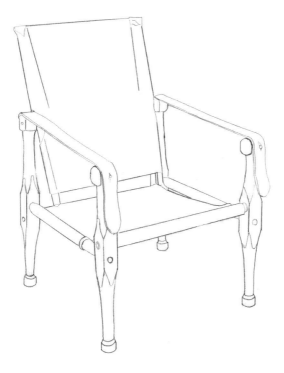

Fig. 7.2 An 1898 Roorkee.

1898 chair and the rear stretcher snapped. It didn't bend and splinter. It snapped like a toothpick.

The problem was two-fold. And this is important so please listen up. The dowel was a stupid dowel. It looked fine from 10', but if you looked closely at the grain you could see that the grain ran out dramatically – over about 6".

Grain "run-out" as it is called, is bad news when it comes to making chairs. Run-out means that the fibers do not extend along the entire length of a piece of wood. Instead, they run out in the middle somewhere. It's a weak spot in wood. In casework, grain run-out is just ugly. In chairmaking, it can kill your design.

So the dowel broke, and I looked like a fool. That was the last dowel I ever used in a Roorkee design. When I returned home to Kentucky, I began testing different stretchers with my friends, both corpulent and stick-figured.

Here's what I found. You can use dowels, but you have to hand-pick them at the store. Don't order them from some catalog. Pick out ones that have zero – or almost zero – grain run-out from end to end. The better solution is to saw (or rive) your own stock. If you are making an oak or ash chair, I recommend you rive the stock for your stretchers, then turn them to 1-1/8" or 1-1/4" in diameter.

If you are using a non-rivable species such as mahogany, then saw the grain as straight as possible. Then turn the stretchers. I saw my stretchers by using a straightedge to mark a line on my rough stock that is parallel to the grain lines of the board. I saw along that line. Then I rip my stretcher material from that line.

This works well. Since I started sawing out my stock this way I have had zero failures – even with people who weigh almost 300 pounds.

In addition to using straight grain, I recommend making the stretchers just a wee bigger in diameter. The originals I examined were about 1" in diameter. By making them 1-1/8" or even 1-1/4" in diameter, they cross some Rubicon of stout-ability. And they don't look much different.

You can make them bigger than 1-1/4", of course. But then they look different – like an elephant trunk instead of the sexy aardvark snout. Don't go overboard.

Leather Design

I am not a leatherworker. Well, I suppose I am now. After making a dozen of these chairs with the help of my shop assistant, Ty Black, I became proficient in cutting and riveting the leather. Even more important than those simple skills, however, is picking the right leather.

Leather, like wood, is a variable and natural product. It moves. It bends. It can be joined. It can do crazy things.

As with wood, the best way to judge leather is in person. You can pull it and judge how much it will stretch. You can get a feel for how it will rip – or fail to rip – when stressed. I prefer to buy my leather in the flesh.

That's not always possible. So here are some guidelines.

For Roorkee chairs, look for a leather that is 7 or 8 ounces in weight. An ounce equals about 1/64" in thickness. So the leather for this chair should be about 1/8" in thickness, maybe a shade less. Thinner leather will stretch and tear.

Some leathers are springier and stretchier than others. You will know this when you pick them up – just like you know if a particular board is hard, soft or rotted.

If you are worried about selecting leather, just get some un-dyed vegetable-tanned leather (the lingo is "veg-tan") that is 7 or 8 ounces in weight. It is stout stuff. It looks like human flesh, which is unsettling. But it is easily colored using dyes and waxes, much like wood.

If you don't want to finish the leather, look for a leather that is "struck through," meaning that it is colored through its entire thickness. Leather that is struck through is no problem to cut or finish. Leather that is not dyed on the inside usually has to be dyed along its edges after you cut it.

In any case, it's easy to get stressed about the leather. Don't. It's a natural material that is easier to cut and work than wood. Go to a local leather store, chat up the owner and you will be fine.

How much leather should you buy? Once again, it will be obvious if you buy

A Taller Roorkee?

I have not strayed from the traditional proportions of the Roorkee when building my versions. Sure, I've altered the turnings and the upholstery, but I haven't messed much with the height of the chair. Or with the cant of the seat.

I had to increase the width and depth of the chair a little to allow the modern body to fit into it. But I haven't wanted to make the chair much taller. Why not? A couple reasons. One is that the chair is supposed to be a low-slung slouchy thing like a Morris chair. It's not for formal dining or office work.

Several customers have asked me to make it tall enough to use at a desk. To do that, I'd have to add 4" to 5" in height. That's dramatic. Not only would it transform the look of the chair, but it would also change the engineering. So I declined.

As noted above, the Roorkee operates at the margins of its materials. Increasing the depth and width of the chair added stress to the stretchers. Adding height would stress the stretchers even more.

I know, I know. I should experiment and find a taller version to make my customers happy. But there have been other design changes I've wanted to explore first, such as making versions of the chair more in the Danish-modern vein.

Feel free to investigate a taller chair. If you do, my recommendation would be to increase the diameter of the stretchers even more.

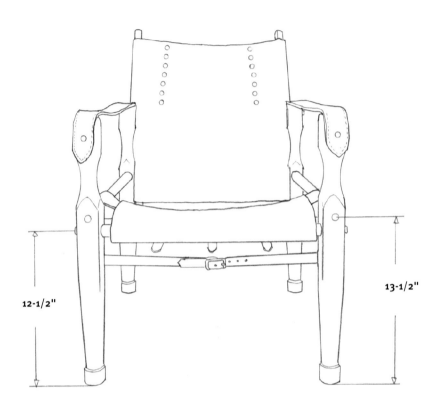

12-1/2"

13-1/2"

Elevation

NO.	PART	SIZES (INCHES)		
		T	W	L
4	Legs	1-7/8	1-7/8	22
4	Stretchers	1-1/4 dia.		23
2	Back pieces	5/8	1-1/2	21
2	5/16" x 3" carriage bolts			
4	5/16" washers			
2	5/16" steel/nylon lock nuts			
4	13mm ball studs (or other size)			
9	3/4" buckles			
1 lb.	No. 9 rivets (3/8" or 1/2" long)			

∾ 1898 ROORKEE ∾

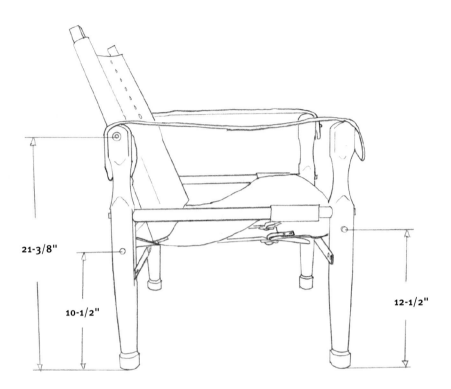

21-3/8"

10-1/2"

12-1/2"

Profile

it in person. If you are ordering it, a "side" will usually generate enough leather for almost two chairs. While you are ordering, also get a side of "veg tan" to make the belting and strapping for the chairs, which also will yield enough belts for everyone in a Catholic family at Christmas.

Spin the Wood

You don't need a lot of wood to make a Roorkee, but the grain needs to be straight. Oak, ash or mahogany are all good traditional choices. The chairs also look smart in walnut or black cherry.

I always turn the legs before making the stretchers or the back pieces. Why? If I ruin a leg on the lathe, it can be converted to a stretcher or a back piece.

Square up the four leg blanks and mark a cabinetmaker's triangle on the bottom of the feet. The point of the triangle should point forward toward the front of the chair. This triangle will guide you throughout construction. It will prevent you from making errors when boring holes. Skip this step at your own peril.

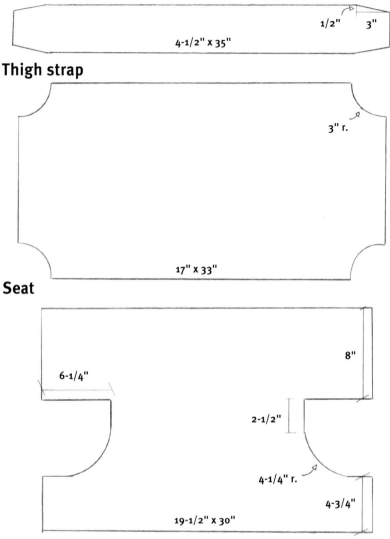

Thigh strap

1/2" 3"

4-1/2" x 35"

3" r.

Seat

17" x 33"

6-1/4"

8"

2-1/2"

4-1/4" r.

4-3/4"

19-1/2" x 30"

Back

Mount a leg in the lathe and turn down the cylinder at the top of the leg to 1-1/4" in diameter. This cylinder is the grip on the chair and is where you will lift the assembled chair when you move it around camp. Take light cuts, especially where the leg changes from square to round. It is easy at the outset to splinter the corners and spoil the leg.

With the grip complete, turn the angled transition from the square to round. This is a tricky bit of work for beginning turners, and it is traditionally done with a skew held with its edge vertical to the work.

Fig. 7.3 A simple template. Here my story stick is sitting on a leg blank chucked into the lathe. Mark out the sections of your turning on the leg blanks.

Fig. 7.4 Begin with the cylinder. If you are going to have a round cylinder at the top of the leg, turn it down with a roughing gouge or a roughing tool, such as this carbide-tipped turning tool.

Fig. 7.5 Tough cut. This transition from square to round is tricky if you are aggressive. It's easy to splinter the exterior surface of the leg. Light cuts, and a tool with a radiused cutting tip, can make it easier for a beginning turner.

Fig. 7.6 Or a curve. Some Roorkee chairs had a curved grip instead of a straight-walled cylinder.

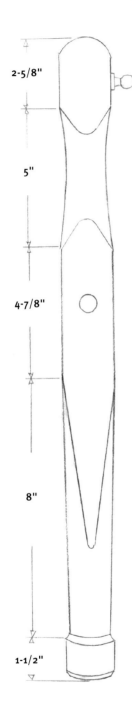

2-5/8"

5"

4-7/8"

8"

1-1/2"

Leg profile

If you are not a skilled turner, you might consider using a carbide-tipped turning tool that has a round tip. Take light cuts and move the tool in a small sweeping arc to make the cut. Light cuts. Again, light cuts.

With the cylindrical grip complete, you are pretty much out of the woods. Now you can turn your attention to the foot. Traditional Roorkees had a small foot. Then the ankle above the foot swells until it makes the transition from round to square again.

Not all Roorkees had feet. Some of the originals had feet that ended in a round taper. These, I suspect, would stick into the turf instead of sitting on top of it.

I like the feet; footless Roorkees look weak and as if they are on tiptoe. To make the feet, first turn down the ankle to its finished diameter of 1-1/4", like the grip above. Make further cuts to create the taper from the ankle to a point about 8" to 8-1/2" above the foot. The exact distance is a moving target.

Again, cutting aggressively can cause your tools to catch the corners and rip out huge chunks of wood, ruining your legs and your day. Take light cuts as you first knock off the corners. With the corners relieved, you can then remove more material.

With all the parts turned, you can sand the round sections while the piece is mounted on the lathe.

Fig. 7.7 Ankle & taper. After turning the ankle, make the gradual taper from the square part of the leg to the foot. Note that I also have started to turn the foot.

Fig. 7.8 Avoid swollen ankles. When cutting the taper above the foot, it's easy to make the taper curved instead of straight. You can sniff out a curve using a ruler (on edge) and some backlighting. Don't go too nuts. If it looks straight, it probably is straight (enough).

Fig. 7.9 Cylinder foot. Instead of a ball-shaped foot, some Roorkees had a straight cylinder for a foot. This one has a small cove at top and a chamfer at the bottom.

Or, if you want a more rough-and-ready Roorkee, skip the sanding and leave (tidy) tool marks.

Remove the leg from the lathe, turn the other three, then prepare to round off the tops of the legs.

Rounded for Comfort

The tops of the legs of most Roorkees are rounded, usually in the shape of a half-circle. The leather arms wrap over the radius, which is nice for your hands and the eyes.

I have a wooden pattern I use to mark the shape, but if you are making only one chair, it's simple work with a compass. Cut the shape on the band saw; remove the tool marks with a rasp or a disc sander. Remember: You don't have to get too precious with the sanding because the tops of the legs will be covered by the leather arm straps.

Likewise, you don't really have to remove the scars from the lathe's drive center. The arms cover it all. Just make sure the overall shape is right; a lumpy curve sticks out.

Fig. 7.10 Around the bend. A thin wooden pattern ensures that all four legs will receive the same shape at top.

Fig. 7.11 Almost done. The tops don't have to be polished like baby's bum, just properly shaped. These legs are almost complete and ready for boring.

Critical Boring Work

The locations of the tapered holes in the legs determine how comfortable the chair is. The holes are also easy to put in the wrong place. Use the triangle on the bottom of your legs to guide the layout process.

To do this layout work, I typically bundle the legs together and set them upright on the workbench. This way I can study the layout marks and ensure they match up with the ruler, my eye and common sense. It is easy to get turned around.

So here's the drill: The stretchers that run from the back legs to the front legs are all at the same height from the floor – 13-1/2" (on centers). The stretchers that run between the two front legs are 12-1/2" from the floor. The stretchers that run between the two rear legs are 10-1/2" from the floor. Simple.

This hole layout creates a chair that encourages you to relax. You can slightly alter the chair's attitude by raising the holes at the rear by 1". That change will make you sit up more at attention.

Lay out the locations of all the holes on the surfaces of the legs that face out. And do the critical boring from the outside surfaces as well. This helps control splintering on visible surfaces.

A tapered socket is cut in two stages. First you drill a hole through the entire leg that's the dimension of the smallest part of the socket. Then you ream out that hole using a tapered reamer.

On the original chair that I studied, the holes were 1/2" in diameter. This works fine and results in a sturdy joint. However, to accommodate the modern hamburger-fed human frame, I increased the diameter of the stretchers to 1 1/8" and 1 1/4". And because of that change, the tooling mandated that I use a 5/8" hole.

This makes the tenon stronger and doesn't change the chair's look too much. I don't like making changes like this to a classic design, but I also don't like it when my customers crash to the floor.

Drill the through-holes in the legs. Use a drill press if you have one. Use great caution if you don't.

Reaming the holes is fairly easy work, either with a drill press or a brace. If you do it with a brace, it helps to have a spotter watch you ream and let you know when you are listing. The other challenge with reaming is knowing when to stop. Small amounts of reaming make significant changes to the hole.

That's why I prefer to use a drill press that has a stop for this work. It's almost impossible to mess up.

However, I have made many chairs without a drill press. It involves some tweaking of the joint, but it isn't terribly difficult.

Ream out the eight holes all to the same depth. Then turn the four stretchers. This is not just a matter of making a homemade dowel. Here are some details.

Fig. 7.12 Clustered & complete. I've bored the through-holes and can now ream them out. When making these chairs, I keep the legs organized like this throughout construction.

Fig. 7.13 Reaming with a brace. Mark your stopping point on the tooling. You want to stop reaming as soon as the tip of the reamer is cutting a 5/8"-diameter hole.

Fig. 7.14 With a drill press. Some reamers can be used in a drill press at a slow speed. This is a quick and easy way to guarantee your hole is straight and true.

The Subtle Stretchers

I wish I had some mahogany-colored titanium for the stretchers. They are the most critical part of the chair and determine whether it will fail or last 110 years and survive a war, a safari or the raising of two rambunctious children.

Once you have your dead-straight-grained stretcher blanks sawn (or split) out, saw or plane them to an octagon and chuck them between centers on the lathe. Turn the stretcher round. Now comes the subtle part of the word "round."

When I turn these stretchers, I make them slightly cigar-shaped along their entire length. The mid-point of the cigar is thickest, 1-1/4" in diameter or a tad more. Then the cigar fades slowly to the point where the taper begins; the stretcher should be a shade less than 1-1/8" about 2" from the ends.

This shape, which is not immediately obvious to the eye, makes the stretchers much stronger. And it makes the tapered tenon easier to create.

The last thing I'll do is turn a rough approximation of the taper on each end of the stretcher. Each tip should be a bit more than 5/8" in diameter. The tenon should start its rough taper about 2" from each end.

This quick-and-dirty turning job saves immense time when shaving the tenon to final shape with a tapered tenon cutter. Commercial tapered tenon cutters are fairly inexpensive and easy to use – they work like a pencil sharpener.

They produce a nice surface when they are sharp and are taking a light cut. They will tear the wood if dull or the cut is too heavy. However, the

Fig. 7.15 Pre-tapered. If you rough in the taper on the lathe, it will greatly reduce the work needed to shape the final taper.

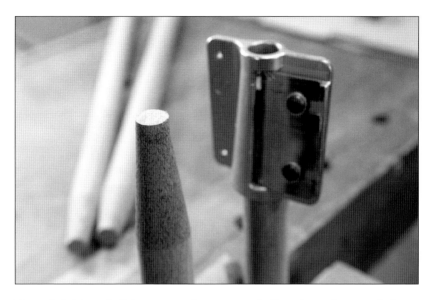

Fig. 7.16 Quick work. Using a tapered tenon cutter is like using a giant pencil sharpener. Focus on keeping the tool centered on the work. If you don't own a tapered tenon cutter, turn the taper on the lathe and adjust it with a spokeshave.

tenon is not a show surface, so it is not necessary to go for a perfect surface.

With the tenons shaved, fit one (a good one) in one of the tapered holes in your legs. Use a square to confirm that the tenon emerges plumb from the leg. Adjust the mortise or the tenon (or both) to make this happen.

Remember: Small adjustments make big changes, both on the tenon and the tapered mortise. If you ream the holes with a drill press, confirmation with a square is nice, but usually unnecessary.

With all eight joints fit, get ready to fit the frame pieces to each other and then make the back.

Two-stick Back

Knock the four stretchers into their holes and the frame should stay together enough to see that everything is in order. The next step is to make the two wooden pieces that will thread through the upholstery and create the back. These back pieces are attached to the back legs of the Roorkee with carriage bolts, washers and wing-nuts (or nylon-sleeved hex nuts).

Each back piece is tapered on one long edge. The back pieces are widest at the middle and taper to 1" wide at either end. These shallow tapers can be made quickly with a jack plane.

Then drill the holes for the bolts. On the back pieces, the holes are in the center of both the width and the length. The matching holes in the rear legs are

Fig. 7.17 Check & check. If you clamp the leg so its exterior surface is flush to the benchtop, it is easy to check the Z-axis of this joint from multiple directions. Get it as close to plumb as possible without shaving the stretcher to a nub or reaming the mortise into a sinkhole.

bored at the centerpoint of the arc on the tops of the leg. When those holes are complete, you can thread the hardware through the holes and affix the two back pieces. Believe it or not, that's all the joinery for the wooden frame of the chair. The remainder of the work is making the seat covers and belting that make the chair a comfortable place to sit.

Finish the Wood; Start the Leather

The finish that looks best on these chairs is simple: garnet shellac followed by a coat of black wax. The shellac gives the wood a warm glow. The black wax gets into the pores and makes mahogany (or oak or ash) look vintage, but not beat up.

Fig. 7.18 Woodwork done. The back pieces have shallow tapers that face the sitter. Attach the back to the frame of the chair using bolts, washers and nuts. The acorn nut shown in the photo is temporary.

For the shellac, I use a 2-pound cut and mix it fresh from flakes. Like any natural product, fresh is better and pure is better. So a new batch of flakes and a quality alcohol makes a nice finish.

I pulverize the flakes before mixing them. There are lots of good and bad ways to do this. Good way: in a plastic bag and with a dead-blow mallet. Bad way: with the food processor in the kitchen.

Apply two coats of shellac (I use an HVLP sprayer), allowing 30 minutes between each coat and sanding between them. After the finish has dried hard and clear, rub on the black wax using a fine abrasive pad. Allow the wax to set up for 10 or 15 minutes, then buff it with a rough cotton cloth.

Fig. 7.19 Before the wax. After two coats of garnet shellac, the mahogany has warmed up considerably. The wax will complete the classic mahogany look.

Words on Herds

Do not be intimidated by the leatherwork. If you are a woodworker with minimal hand skills and you know what sharp is, you will breeze through this leather-working project. Sure, there are a couple unfamiliar tools (rivet setter? skiving knife?), but you will pick up the basics in just a few minutes.

Like woodworking, leatherwork is all about cutting the material, joining it so it holds together and finishing it so it looks good.

When it comes to cutting the leather, you can cut up all the stock with a sharp utility knife. One additional tool I might recommend is a leather-slitting tool, a simple and inexpensive appliance that makes all the straps you need for the chair.

I usually begin by making all the straps and belting for a chair. The straps hold the upholstery tight and keep the legs from twisting out of their sockets when you grind into the seat. You need about 12' of 3/4"-wide belting for each chair, and I make it from 7- to 8-ounce vegetable-tanned leather.

A good place to get started with leatherworking is to make the belting that goes between the left and right legs. These work just like the kind of belt you wear; there's a buckle and a strap (the "bite"), which threads through the buckle and is punched with holes.

The only real difference is that the ends of the straps are screwed to the legs with brass screws and finishing washers.

Cut a piece of belting so it is about 14" long. To attach it to the buckle it is

Fig. 7.20 A slitter. This leather-slitting tool works a bit like a table saw. You move the fence of the tool away from the cutter (3/4" in this case) and feed the leather between the fence and cutter and it will make leather straps all day long. You can usually cut up an entire side of a cow into ribbons before resharpening or replacing the cutter.

best to thin the thickness of the belting a little where it loops back and is riveted to itself. Thinning the leather is traditionally done with a special skiving knife. You can do it with a utility knife if you are deliberate. Thin the last 2" so it tapers to about half the original thickness.

Now punch out the hole that will receive the prong of the buckle. There are special tools that will do this all in one whack, or you can use a leather punch to define the ends of the hole you need and join the two holes with your knife.

To attach the belting to the buckle, you'll need to rivet it. The rivets I use are simply two pieces of metal that fasten together and pinch the leather tight. Traditional rivets are made of copper and have a post and a "burr," which is, essentially, a washer.

To install a rivet, you punch a tight-fitting hole through the two pieces of leather you want to join. Then you push the post through both pieces of leather and press the washer (the burr) over the post. Use a rivet setter to drive the burr down onto the leather. With nail nippers, snip off the excess post; leave about 1/16" of the post above the washer.

Place the rivet on a steel plate and use your rivet setter to peen the copper post. This locks the rivet tight. You can then shape the rivet with a regular hammer.

There are dozens of other kinds of rivets for leather and metalworking.

Fig. 7.21 Punched & ready. Here you can see all the holes punched in the leather belting before looping one end around the buckle and riveting the loop.

One of the other common ones you will encounter for leather are sometimes called rapid rivets. They are easier to install than traditional rivets and look somewhat like a button. I've built a couple chairs with these and they work fine. I, however, prefer the look and strength of the traditional copper rivets. They are worth the extra effort.

Before riveting the strap around the buckle, wet the area of the leather that needs to bend. Water makes the leather more pliable. Insert the prong of the buckle (make sure it's facing the correct direction) onto the strap and rivet it tight. Use one or two rivets. It's your call.

For the mating strap, called the "bite," all you have to do is punch some holes that are big enough to receive the buckle's prong. Space these about

Fig. 7.22 A bit slower. Riveting with copper rivets takes a couple extra steps. Punch the hole. Push the post through the holes. Set the washer. Snip the post and peen the post. Installed correctly, rivets are remarkably strong.

1/2" apart. Lay out five or six with dividers and punch them out.

Congratulations. You have a functional belt. Now all you have to do is attach it to the legs. Position the belt so the buckle will end up in the middle of the space between the back legs and about 2" or so below the stretcher. Fasten each end of the belting to the inside of the leg using two No. 8 x 1-1/2" brass screws and finishing washers. If there is any excess leather, snip it off with a knife.

Repeat this process for the strap between the front legs of the chair.

The Seat Covers

The bulk of the leather in this project involves the seat covers. In this chair, there are three pieces that make up the seat:

The back. This piece is a rectangle that is notched so it can wrap around where the two back pieces join the legs. The leather back can be held in place with rivets, buckles, stitches or some combination of joinery.

The seat. The seat is also a rectangle that wraps around the front and rear stretchers. It can be riveted, sewn or buckled in place. I recommend buckles so that you can take up any slack that develops when the leather stretches.

The thigh strap. Some chairs had this long and somewhat skinny strap that ran from the left stretcher to the right and sat below your thighs. I was turned on to this important piece of leather by Australian woodworker Greg

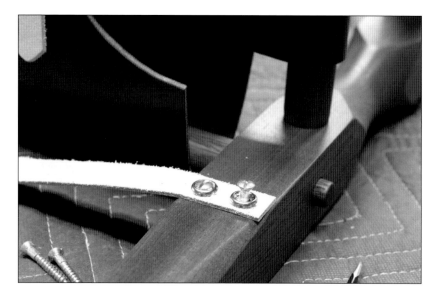

Fig. 7.23 Belting attached. Though these screws are hidden on the inside of the chair, I still like to use nice slotted brass screws and finishing washers, which give the screw some more grip.

Miller, who made Roorkee chairs commercially. The thigh strap is an efficient and effective bit of engineering. It should, in my opinion, be buckled so that you can take out the slack.

I have provided sizes for these pieces, but do not use them except as a general guide. Instead, take the measurements from your chair. If you shaved or reamed too much or too little, the size of the seat can change.

Here are some guidelines. You want the back to be almost as wide as the back pieces are long. If your back pieces are 21" long, make the back 19-1/2" to 20" wide so the wooden back pieces will poke out a bit. You can make the leather back piece a little narrower so the wooden back pieces protrude as much as 1", which looks correct on some old chairs. On later chairs, such as the Safari Chair, the wooden back was covered entirely by leather.

The length of the back should be long enough to wrap around the wooden back bits and overlap itself by about 3" or a little more. I'd say 30" long is a good starting place.

Then you need to cut rectangular notches in the leather back. These notches allow the wooden back pieces to mate with the legs. A good starting point is shown in the illustrations. Making the notch a little taller won't hurt. Making the notch a little too small will cause lots of problems with the leather binding against the frame. The notch shown in the drawing allows extra room. If you use buckles on the back, make the bite pieces about 13" long.

Fig. 7.24 Do it on the floor. Hardboard templates are an inexpensive way to more easily make several chairs. When I cut out a set of leather pieces, I kneel on the template parts to hold them in place.

The seat should be wide enough to fill the space between the left and right legs with a little room for the wooden back pieces to come down. A width of 16-3/4" to 17" is ideal. A little narrower will give you some room to shift and wiggle the chair's components together.

The seat's length should be enough that the leather can wrap around the front stretchers and make room for attaching straps and buckles. If you have enough leather on hand, 37" is a good starting place, though you could get away with less (33") if the bovine demands it. (I used 33" when making these chairs in Germany where I was plagued by smaller cows.) The bites for the seat pieces should be 17" long or so with a shorter seat.

And finally, the thigh strap. It's 4-1/2" wide and 35" long. This length allows you to wrap it around the stretchers on the sides and add buckles and

Fig. 7.25 Shortcut. If you plan to make a lot of these chairs, purchase a special punch that will make the oval orifice needed for the buckle. The leather piece is 5-1/2", folded over in the middle of its length and moistened in the mouth. Yum.

straps. The bites for the thigh strap should be about 13" long.

To cut out the leather, I recommend you make templates out of an inexpensive and thin material, such as MDF or tempered hardboard, even if you are making only one chair. These templates allow you to shift them around on the hide like puzzle pieces to try several strategies for getting the maximum yield from a hide. Plus, when you are ready, you can just trace around the template with a knife to cut out your piece.

With the pieces cut out, it's a matter of riveting them and adding the belting. It is not any different than making the belting between the legs – except that you rivet the belting to the leather (or canvas) instead of screwing it to the wood.

The seat needs three or four buckles. The thigh strap needs two. For the back, you can attach the two lower tabs using one buckle or two.

The Arm Rests

The biggest challenge with attaching the arm straps is finding the hardware that screws into the legs and allows you to button down the leather straps. I finally settled on using 13mm ball socket studs, which are used to attach gas struts to

Fig. 7.26 Punching tool. The rotary punch is a fast way of making lots of holes (in different sizes) for rivets or holes for buckles.

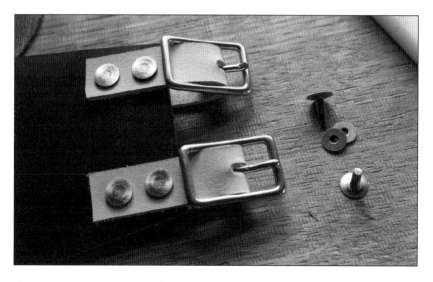

Fig. 7.27 Flat & smooth. Each rivet has a flat face and a face with a bump. Here you can see the flat face. You want this face to be on the most visible part of the belt.

automotive bodies – these are the struts that hold up the windows on the back of a pickup truck's camper top.

You can find them at general supply stores, such as Grainger and McMaster-Carr. They come in a variety of sizes and with different post sizes and lengths.

Fig. 7.28 Set the burr. After you place the burr on the post of the rivet, you need to push it down to pinch the leather bits. Do this with a rivet setter. Most rivet setters have a hole designed for this operation.

Fig. 7.29 One back route. Here I am riveting the leather back pieces. The tape marks where the folded leather end should sit when everything is complete. All of the layout here is done by eye and with the assistance of dividers.

Fig. 7.30 Tapping. It's best to tap the hole for the 13mm ball studs. If you don't have a tap you can make do with an undersized hole – and perhaps a dab of epoxy.

Don't get too worked up about picking the right size. This piece of metal doesn't get too much stress. What's more important is that you own the right drill bit and tap so you can screw the ball stud into the leg.

(Side note, if you don't own a tap set, you can usually get away with drilling a hole that you can tap with the threads of the ball studs. You should experiment with different hole sizes in scrap wood that is the same species as your chair.)

Drill and tap the holes for the four ball studs. Alternately, you can screw the arm straps to the rear legs (it's traditional). I typically see three screws arranged in a triangle pattern on each strap. If you do that, then you need only two 13mm ball studs for each chair.

The leather for the arm rests is 1-3/4" wide. If your leather is thin, consider doubling up two pieces and gluing them face to face using a leather cement such as Original Barge Cement. Or you can glue and stitch them.

To attach the leather to the studs, use a 1/4" drive punch to make a hole in the correct spot. Then slit the leather a tad with a knife so the hole will button securely over the 13mm ball stud.

Make the leather for the arms a little tighter than you think you should. It will loosen up. But don't make it so tight that the legs start to tilt. If you do that, you are headed for a broken stretcher.

From the first to the last, Roorkee chairs are a balancing act of materials and joinery. Hit the sweet spot, and you will end up with a chair that will last forever. Get sloppy, and you will end up on a pile of splinters and leather on your floor.

Fig. 7.31 Screws instead of studs. These No. 8 x 1-1/2" brass screws with finishing washers are a simple and strong way to secure the armrest to the rear legs.

Stripping Zinc from Hardware

For the hardware that joins the back pieces to the legs, I buy inexpensive zinc-plated hardware and strip off the zinc with citric acid. It takes only about an hour, is very safe and makes the hardware look nice and old.

Citric acid is not lemon juice. You can buy it at health-food stores, where it is sold for canning or freeze-drying foods. It's a white powder that, when mixed with water, creates a weak acid bath for your hardware. You can safely dunk your hands in it.

I usually mix it 1:10 with warm water. I first clean any oil off the hardware and drop it in the bath. Stir it occasionally. If the acid stops working, add more powder.

Once the stripping is complete, wash the hardware in water and rub it with some oil. Any oil will do.

Oh, and if nothing happens, chances are your hardware isn't plated with zinc. It's probably nickel, chrome or stainless steel. Stripping those is no fun.

FIG. 7.32. A Kaare Klint Safari Chair in
ebonized mahogany.

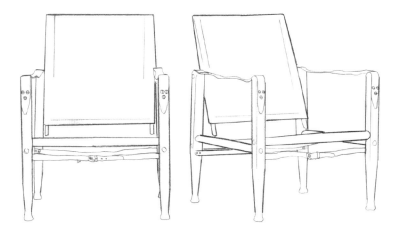

Kaare Klint Safari Chair

The original 19th-century Roorkee chair looks at home on safari. Whereas the mid-century Kaare Klint "Safari Chair" looks right in the home.

What is surprising – no shocking – is how closely the Klint chairs mimic the original Roorkee of 50 years earlier. They are so similar that it's almost not fair to call the Safari Chair anything more than a minor evolution from the original.

Here are some details:

The legs of the original were 1-1/2" square and 22-1/2" long. The Klint chair legs are 1-9/16" square and 22" long.

The stretchers of the original were 1" to 1-1/8" in diameter. The Klint chair has stretchers that are 1-1/4" in diameter that are clearly cigar-shaped, like those described above.

The seat height is also similar between the original and the Klint. On the original, the front of the seat was 12" from the floor and the back of the seat is 10-1/2" from the floor. On the Klint, the front stretcher is 12" from the floor and the rear is 9-1/2" from the floor. The back is virtually identical.

There are some interesting differences. Klint moved the side stretchers down. This gives the chair a sleeker look in my opinion and, engineering-wise, reduces the leverage on the side stretchers. However, it reduces the effectiveness of the thigh strap.

Klint also removed the handles at the top of the legs, which is probably the most visible difference, but it has little to do with how the chair sits or works.

Typically, the Klint chairs had their arm straps screwed to the legs – not buttoned. I have seen a couple Klint chairs that use snaps instead of screws.

I have built three Klint-style chairs and use all the same dimensions as for the original 1898 Roorkee. The only significant differences are the simplified turnings and the way the arm straps attach to the legs.

Fig. 8.1. A strong trunk in mahogany
with 'riveted' corners.

CHAPTER 8

STRONG TRUNK

One of the more common pieces of campaign furniture is the simple trunk, sometimes also called a "strong chest," "traveling chest" or "barracks chest." The one shown in this chapter, however, has some unusual details you should be aware of. More about those oddities in a few paragraphs.

Trunks typically have square ends – both the height and depth of the trunk can be roughly 15" to 25". In general, they are somewhere between 25" to 40" wide. The chests are frequently dovetailed at the corners and bound with brass corners and other brass straps. Despite the dovetails, many of the lids and bottoms of trunks were merely nailed to the carcase. It is not unusual to find a trunk with a lid or bottom that has a split.

The trunks almost always had a lock or hasp to protect the contents.

Many of the trunks were raised on some sort of foot. The foot could be as simple as a sledge (sometimes called sled) foot – just a square of wood – all the way to a complex bracket foot.

Inside, many trunks had a small till with a lid, much like a typical household chest. This till stored small items and its lid served as a stop to hold the trunk's lid open. The chests are typically made from mahogany, oak, teak and camphorwood, which naturally repels moths.

Fig. 8.2 A 'rivet.' This piece of early campaign hardware is held in with screws that then had their heads filed off flush to the pull. This feature shows up on other pieces and even on English infill handplanes.

The trunk shown here is typical in many of its attributes except for the joinery at the corners. Instead of dovetails, I have chosen an uncommon (but definitely reliable) type of joinery found on trunks from the West Indies.

That's a Rivet?

I first encountered this joint while haunting antique stores on King Street in Charleston, S.C. One of the trunks there had a series of brass circles that ran in a line up each corner. At first it looked like brass inlay, which is a common feature of some Anglo-Indian campaign pieces.

Instead of decoration, the brass circles turned out to be the joinery.

The dealer, who had imported campaign furniture from the West Indies for decades, explained that some collectors referred to that joint as a "rivet." He explained that the rivet was nothing more than a brass screw that had been driven in so its head was still proud. Then the screw head was filed flush to the carcase, eliminating the slot.

It's a surprisingly simple and (I think) attractive way to make a strong joint that looks a lot better than having 12 wooden screw plugs lined up on the corners.

This approach shows up in other applications in the woodworking field. Sometimes, screw heads are filed flush with a piece of hardware. And if you've

Fig. 8.3 Typically English. This small trunk features blind dovetails at the corners, brass corners, chest lifts and a strong lock.

ever seen infill handplanes, you know it was common for the maker to screw in the wooden infills and the lever cap then file off the heads – making for a clean sidewall of the tool.

This trunk is based on several smaller English examples I've studied that were dovetailed. But instead of the dovetails, I substituted "rivets" as the joinery to make the trunk look more like one from the West Indies. If you want a more English look, cut through- or full-blind dovetails at the corners. The other decorative details, such as the brass corners and bracket feet, pretty much remain the same.

Almost a Butt Joint

The joinery of the trunk is as simple as a modern kitchen cabinet. The ends are captured by 5/16"-deep x 5/8"-wide rabbets cut on the ends of the front and back pieces. This corner joint is first glued then later screwed. The bottom is captured in a groove plowed in the ends, front and back.

The lid is built a lot like the case below. The ends are glued into rabbets in the front and back pieces. The lid is then nailed on top of that assembly.

When building the carcase, there are two basic paths you can follow. You can build the entire chest and lid as one unit then saw the lid free from the carcase. Or you can build the lid and carcase separately.

I took a path between these extremes. I cut the joints on all the parts. Then I ripped the lid parts free from the carcase parts. I assembled the lid and carcase separately. Why? I don't like pushing a big assembled carcase over a table saw. But all three approaches work. Choose one you like.

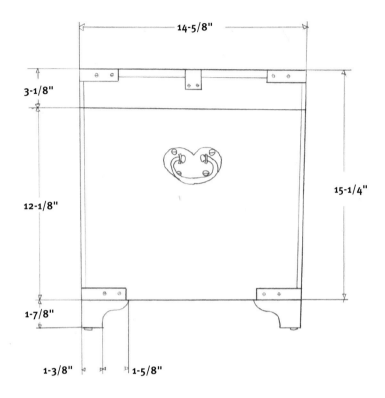

14-5/8"

3-1/8"

12-1/8"

15-1/4"

1-7/8"

1-3/8"   1-5/8"

Profile

❧ STRONG TRUNK ❧

NO.	PART	SIZES (INCHES)		
		T	W	L
2	Front & back	5/8	14-3/4	26
2	Ends	5/8	14-3/4	14
1	Top	5/8	14-5/8	26
1	Bottom	5/8	14-3/4	25-1/4
8	Bracket feet	5/8	1-7/8	3
4	Glue blocks	5/8	5/8	2

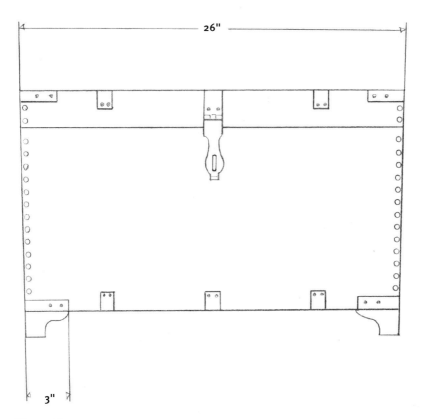

Elevation

No matter how you proceed, the first step is to cut the rabbets on the ends of the front and back pieces. The rabbets are 5/16" deep x 5/8" wide. If you do them by hand, don't forget to drop the nickers on your plane.

No matter how you cut the rabbets, confirm that they are square before calling them done.

After cutting the rabbets, I ripped the lid pieces free from the carcase pieces and marked all my parts so the grain would match at the seam when the trunk was assembled. The cutting list includes a 1/8" allowance for the kerf.

For the bottom of the carcase, I chose to let it float in a groove in the front, back and ends. On some trunks, the bottom was merely nailed on. Allowing it to float in a groove reduces the chance that the bottom will split.

I plowed a 1/4" x 1/4" groove in the front, back and ends. The groove is 5/16" deep, just like the rabbet. Then I cut a mating tongue on all four edges of the bot-

Fig. 8.4 Rabbeted ends. The cross-grain rabbets wrap around the ends. I cut these joints using a dado stack in my table saw.

Fig. 8.5 Free lid. I cut the rabbets first then ripped the lid pieces free from the carcase pieces. Cutting rabbets on narrow parts can be difficult.

Fig. 8.6 Grooved & ready. Here you can see how the bottom slips into place in its groove in the ends, front and back.

tom board. The bottom should be given a little space to expand and contract in its width. You can fit it tight in the groove along its length.

Once you get all the joints cut, that is an excellent time to clean up all the surfaces with a handplane, especially the inside surfaces. Do your best to remove any machine marks on the outside of the case now as well, because the screws in this project will make your life difficult. You want the exterior to always be close to finished.

Glue-up then Screw-up

You could glue and screw the entire case together, but that would involve a lot of planning and rehearsing and (I think) luck. My preference is to glue the case together, let everything cure and then add the screws.

There is a trick to gluing up a carcase with joints that are made up of crappy grain orientation – face grain that is joined to end grain. The trick is to fool the end grain into thinking it is face grain.

I learned this trick from Dale Zimmerman, a retired senior technical specialist at Franklin International. Dale has been studying glue and messing with it for decades and has the numbers to back up the technique. I have been using it for years now and know that it works.

One reason that joints involving end grain are weak is because the end grain soaks up the adhesive from the joint line, starving the bond. The trick is to clog the pores of the end grain with glue so that they cannot suck up the glue.

Here's how you do it: Spread a thin layer of wet glue (any kind) on the end-grain portion of the joint. Let it sit for one full minute. The surface should become dry in some areas, which is evidence that the end grain is indeed sucking up the adhesive.

Then apply a second coat of wet glue over the first and put your parts together. The clogged pores should allow the glue to now make a very decent bond with the wood.

So do this with the carcase parts. Smear glue on the end grain. Wait. Apply more glue. Clamp the carcase parts together. Check the carcase to ensure it is square. Let it sit until the glue has cured.

Postpone the screwing as long as possible. It's better that way.

Add the Lid

Remove the machine marks from all the lid pieces and get ready to glue it up. Here's how: Clean any dried bits of glue off the carcase with a chisel and cover the top rim of the case with masking tape. The tape will prevent any glue squeeze-out from the lid from sticking to your carcase.

Glue up the lid parts using the same routine as you did on the carcase (glue, wait, glue again). Then clamp the lid parts in position on top of the carcase. Your clamps should be able to hold the lid pieces together and hold them in position on the carcase. This clamping strategy ensures your lid will be the same shape as the carcase below it.

Still, check everything for square. Your lid should be just as square (or out-of-square) as the carcase you glued up earlier.

Let the glue cure. Cut the top piece to final size, which should be just a bit oversized – you want to have to trim back some overhang.

The joint between the lid and the top is critical. Do it wrong and your top will crack open with seasonal humidity changes.

Here's the right way: The joint is just glue and nails. Use glue along the front edge of the lid and about one-third down the ends of the lid. Then nail the top in place using *4d* cut headless brads (or *4d* wire brads if you prefer).

This strategy will keep the top flush at the front of the lid, which is the most visible part of the chest. The nails will allow the top to move and shift. But all the wood movement will be to the rear of the lid assembly.

A Simple Seal

Some of these trunks had to be airtight or watertight, especially the ones designed for sailors. So some would be lined with zinc or have fancy seals to keep the trunks from sinking if they wound up in the ocean. This trunk has a simple seal.

Fig. 8.7 I feel dry. You can see how the end grain of the end pieces has soaked up this hide glue after less than 60 seconds. A second coat of glue will make the joint stronger.

Fig. 8.8 Clamp off the edge. Push the end of the carcase off your workbench to clamp across the joint. Try to keep the jaws of the clamps positioned over the joint line only.

Fig. 8.9 Two clamps & done. The lid parts sit on top of some masking tape. Clamps (not shown) hold the lid pieces together and to the carcase below.

Fig. 8.10 Tricky. Glue only the front part of the lid to the top, but nail it all around. That's the best strategy in this situation.

Fig. 8.11 Nail & set. I clamped the front edge of the top and lid together while I nailed the top down all around. The clamps keep everything in place while you do your nailing.

However, even the basic trunks would have a simple seal to help keep out bugs and dirt. This seal is a raised lip on the interior of the carcase. Usually it was mitered and applied to the inside of the case or it was integral to the front, back and ends.

I chose to make the liner from 1/8"-thick mahogany that I mitered and glued to the inside of the carcase. The liner sticks up 1/4" from the carcase.

To make the liner, I mitered the parts using a miter box and saw. Then I shot the ends on a miter shooting board. Finally, I glued and clamped the parts of the seal to the carcase.

Screwing Times 60

Adding the screws at this point is much easier than trying it when the glue is wet and the parts are sliding around. Before you screw this up, be sure to mark on the carcase all the outlines of the corner hardware you will add. Having the outlines – even in pencil – will prevent you from putting a screw where it shouldn't be.

The first step is layout. Strike a line that is 5/16" from the end of the front and back pieces. This is the line where your screws will go. Then get your dividers and the screws you plan to use.

I used No. 10 x 1-1/4" oval-head brass screws from a boatbuilding supplier. Stores that cater to boatbuilders have a good selection of fasteners.

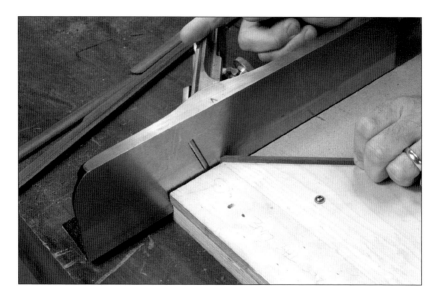

Fig. 8.12 Shoot the miters. If you set the plane to take a light cut, you won't have any trouble with the outside edge of the seal's miter splintering.

Fig. 8.13 Glue & clamps. Here you can see the seal poking up above the rim of the carcase. That's all it takes to keep out the bugs.

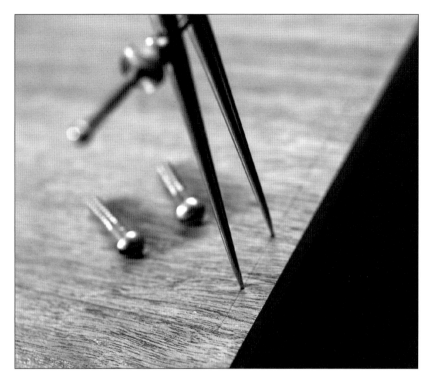

Fig. 8.14 Walk it off. On the chests I examined, the spacing between each screw was greater than the diameter of one screw. So don't space them too tightly.

Then I decided on the spacing for the screws. After looking at several chests from the West Indies, I decided to measure the diameter of the head of the screw. Then I spaced the screws so there would be a space equal to 1-1/2 head diameters between each head.

Confused? Step it off with dividers and line up some screws on your chest (start at the back) to find the right spacing. In the end, I set my dividers to 13/16" and walked down the chest to leave 13 holes on each corner.

With the holes pricked in the carcase on all four corners, you can drill the pilot holes and just a shade of a countersink. I used a bit that drilled the pilot and countersink in one operation, and it had a stop collar so that it made the same countersink every time. This is quite handy.

Before you start drilling on your trunk, I recommend making a couple test holes in some scrap. You want just a wee bit of a countersink so that the bugle-shaped head of the screw bites down into the countersink and compresses the wood just a tad. This will make for a seamless surface between the brass and wood. A too-deep countersink will look terrible; either part of the screw's slot will remain or you will have a gap around the brass.

Fig. 8.15 Tiny countersinks. Set the stop on your bit so it makes just a shade of a countersink – less than 1/16" deep. This will allow the screw to compress the wood a bit and leave a seamless joint.

Fig. 8.16 And screw. Drive the No. 10 screws in so the bottom of the slot is co-planar to the carcase. That will result in the least amount of brass to remove.

Then drive in the screws. Use a little lubricant (I use paraffin or beeswax) and drive the screws in so the bottom of the slot is coplanar to the surface of the carcase. Do not allow the bottom of the slot to go below the surface of the carcase. That's bad.

Filing the Screw Heads

Leveling the brass screw heads is more tedious than it is difficult. I tried a variety of ways to speed up the process, such as a metal-cutting blade in a Fein Multi-Master, a hacksaw and various kinds of files.

Those solutions worked. Kinda. But the Multi-Master scored the wood unacceptably, as did the hacksaw.

The best solution was to use a file – either a laminate file or a multi-cut file. And instead of using it freehand, I did most of the work with the file in a jig that prevented an errant stroke from decimating my mahogany.

The jig is simple. It's a chunk of wood that I cut a rabbet into. The rabbet is the width of the file. The depth of the rabbet is the thickness of the file plus some carpet tape. Then I glued a fence to the block to keep the jig at 90°.

Fig. 8.17 Filing jig. An offcut of poplar and some carpet tape makes the basic jig. Add a fence to the jig to make it a can't-miss affair.

Fig. 8.18 Push or pull. By orienting the file one way or the other, you can use the jig in a pushing or pulling position. Both work.

Fig. 8.19 Slow & steady. After 10 minutes of filing, you will reach the bottom of the slot. Then you have to clean up your work deliberately in order to avoid gouging the surrounding wood.

Fig. 8.20 A little abrasive action. When you reach the screw slot, you can move things along a little faster with a random-orbit sander and some #120-grit sandpaper.

Fig. 8.21 Final filing. The sander will eat away more wood than brass. So after sanding, use a file to level the tops of the screws with a few finishing strokes.

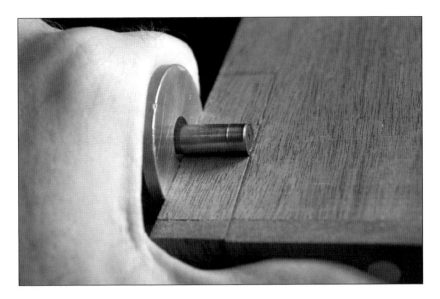

Fig. 8.22 Gauge the height. Use a cutting gauge to mark in the exact height of the brass corner.

To file the screw heads, clamp the trunk's carcase to your bench then push the filing jig across the screw heads. It took me about 30 minutes per corner to file the screws, so take your time and don't try to rush the job.

Every few minutes, clean the file (rubbing chalk across its teeth helps keep it clean), and vacuum up the brass filings from the work.

When you reach the bottom of the screws' slots, you can switch to some power sanding to help move things along. I used #120-grit sandpaper in an orbital sander to remove a little brass and wood. The sander will remove more wood than brass, leaving the brass bits a bit higher – like a mosquito bite.

Use a fine file to dress down the bumps until the surface feels smooth. Sand a little more then file a little more if necessary. The last step should be filing the last little bit of brass bumpiness away with a fine file and gentle stokes.

Install the Brass Corners & Hasp

Like most campaign pieces, this trunk has a lot of brass bits. It's easy to feel overwhelmed by the amount of mortising required for a typical piece. And it's easy to take shortcuts – to skip a few pieces of brass or (shiver) install the brass proud of the carcase.

I've done both of these things, and it's not worth the long-term regret.

The trick to doing this right is simple: Simply commit to it. Schedule a few hours in the shop to install brass, and you will find that the work isn't bad at all. For example, I installed all the brass on this trunk in four hours of concen-

Fig. 8.23 Gauge the length. With a second gauge, cut in the exact length of the corner hardware.

trated work. No machines or power tools. And no interruptions.

I prefer to install brasses by hand. While I might waste away some of the material with a drill or a router at times, I always come back to doing most of the work by hand. It is direct and difficult to screw up.

The photos here explain the steps and show the process better than words. The basic drill is this: Use a cutting gauge to slice in all the extents of the hardware. Chop up the waste with a chisel, taking care not to split the work with too-aggressive mallet whacks. Then snowplow the waste using a small router plane that is set to the final depth. In some cases, it pays to pare out the waste with a chisel first.

Bracket Feet

You don't have to put feet on your trunk. Some trunks didn't have feet. Some had feet that were added later. Some had simple sledge feet. All those solutions are fine.

I put bracket feet on mine to raise the trunk off the floor a bit and give it a couple curves. If I were getting on a ship for India, however, I'd skip the bracket feet because they would surely get soaked or snapped off.

These bracket feet are about as simple as they come. They are mitered at the corners and reinforced with 5/8"-square glue blocks, which stick 1/8" below the mitered bracket pieces.

The brackets have a simple ogee cut into them – pretty standard stuff. To make life easier, I assembled each foot separately, then attached them to the case with glue and nails. This strategy allows you to adjust the parts until the

Fig. 8.24 Chop with care. At times you will chop a combination of face grain and end grain. If you get too aggressive, you can split both. Always begin with light chops until you have a feel for the grain.

Fig. 8.25 Rout it. A small router plane can remove the waste in one pass if your chisel chops have been strategic. Plan your cuts so the waste supports the tool's sole for as long as possible.

miter is perfect and the feet are flush to the carcase.

I made a pattern of the foot shape on a piece of scrap and traced that onto my mahogany parts, which were left over-long to make them easier to clamp and work. Cut the ogee shape; refine the shape with rasps and abrasives. Then cut the miters to free the piece from the longer piece of wood.

Repeat the process until you have eight mitered pieces. Then cut the four 5/8" x 5/8" x 2" glue blocks. Gluing the mitered corners is easy if you have some packing tape. Stick the mating foot pieces so their miters touch. Apply a smear of glue. Wait a minute. Apply more. Then fold the miters together.

Nail and glue the glue block in the corner and use some more tape to hold the miter closed until the glue cures.

Installing the bracket feet is straightforward. Simply glue and clamp them to the case. It's a long-grain joint and there is no cross-grain. So there is no need for a

A Hammer Helps Some Installations

Some campaign hardware has sharp inside corners – usually because it was welded or cast that way. Other pieces have rounded inside corners because the hardware was bent over a form.

If your hardware has rounded corners, you have to shape the wood to match the hardware. (I know: Duh.) You can do this with a chisel, which works. But I found it was faster to do it with a small hammer.

I cut a quick chamfer with a chisel then hammered all the corners into a rounded shape.

Try it before you reject the idea.

Fig. 8.26 Shape, then cut. First cut the ogee shape into the foot when it is part of a longer piece. This makes it easier to clamp and work. Then miter the corner.

Fig. 8.27 Tape is a great clamp. I use packing tape to glue the miters together. Apply glue, wait, then apply more. Then tape the assembly so the miter is tight.

Fig. 8.28 Taped & done. Here you can see the glue block in place and sticking out a wee bit from the bottom of the bracket feet. This is all the clamping you need with these feet.

fastener to keep the glue line strong. That said, feet take a heap of abuse, and it is usually a good idea to screw the foot to the carcase in two spots to strengthen the foot against an impact or moisture that could weaken your glue.

Finishing Up

As much as I don't like power sanding, this project is ideal for it because of the screw joinery.

When building this trunk, I tried to avoid power sanding by first planing up all the panels, assembling the case then filing the screw heads back. With a file alone, however, it was quite tricky to get the screw heads flush without dinging the carcase. But it was quite easy with a random-orbit sander. So I leveled the brass first with #120 grit then finished up the case with #150-grit abrasive.

After sanding all the surfaces, I finished the case with two coats of garnet shellac, one coat of dull lacquer and a coat of black paste wax.

The shellac gave the wood a nice color, the lacquer gave it a nice sheen and the black wax filled in the pores and toned the wood so it didn't look shockingly new. It's a simple finishing schedule that I use all the time with open-pored woods such as mahogany. For close-pored woods, I skip the black wax because I don't think it adds much.

Fig. 8.29 Glue (plus screws). Some glue and a clamp is all you need to keep the foot in place. However, adding a couple screws is ideal.

Fig. 9.1. A folding field desk in teak.

type
CHAPTER 9
FIELD DESK

F urniture pieces that folded flat were common items among British officers. Chairs, card tables, bookshelves, beds and coat racks were just some of the fold-flat items that cabinetmakers and furniture companies made for Great Britain's mobile empire.

When I selected the projects for this book, I wanted to include a piece of furniture that folded flat. However, the most common piece of flat-folding campaign furniture is a chair. And chairs can be intimidating for many woodworkers – even chairs that don't fold up.

So instead, I decided to build this simple Regency-style folding field desk, which was constructed during the reign of William IV (1830-1837). The desk uses the same folding mechanism used by campaign chairs and some folding bookshelves, but this project is much less intimidating because all the joinery is 90°. This allows you to focus on how the mechanism works. Once you master this simple table, I think you'll have no problem seeing how the same principles work with a chair, bed or other frame-based piece of furniture.

The field desk is made up of two components: the tabletop and the base. The top is three pieces of wood that are joined by hinges. The two end leaves fold up to protect the central desktop and reduce the top to half its unfolded length.

Fig. 9.2 Ready for travel. The flat-folding field desk shown in pieces.

One unusual aspect of the desktop is that the hinges have their barrels sticking up a bit above the top. This is a bit annoying for a desk.

There are alternate ways to hinge the three pieces of the top, including using four card-table hinges, which would be installed on the long edges of the top pieces. Note that a desktop hinge (the kind used for a drop-front secretary) won't work here. The pivot point of the barrel is too low to allow the leaves to fold closed and flat. You need a third pivoting leaf in the middle.

The table base folds flat with the assistance of six butt hinges, which regulate the folding action of the four side apron pieces. It takes a few minutes to understand how the mechanism works, but once you get it, you'll get it forever.

This folding mechanism is surprisingly easy to install. Four of the butt hinges are simply screwed to the inside surfaces of the aprons. The other two butt hinges are installed in shallow mortises in the side aprons.

So what keeps the table open and standing sturdily? The interface between the top and the base.

On the original table, the four legs of the base each had a brass pin that projected above the top of each leg. The bullet-shaped pin was embedded in a brass plate that was mortised into the end of each leg.

The bullet-shaped pins mated with four holes in the underside of the folding desktop. The holes were bound in brass. It's an ingenious mecha-

Fig. 9.3 Four bastards. See how the annular rings run through the legs at 45° (or thereabouts)? That's bastard grain, and this annular-ring orientation ensures your legs will look pleasing from all points in a room or a tent.

❦ Field Desk ❦

NO.	PART	SIZES (INCHES)		
		T	W	L
4	Legs	2	2	32
2	Long aprons	7/8	3-1/2	50-3/4
4	Short aprons	7/8	3-1/2	10-1/4
2	Small tops	3/4	24	13-1/2
1	Large top	3/4	24	26-7/8
2	Short cleats	3/4	3/4	6
2	Long cleats	3/4	3/4	12

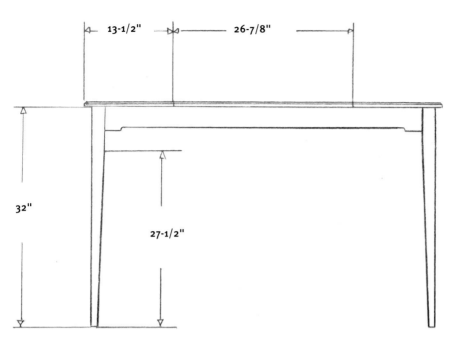

13-1/2" 26-7/8"

32"

27-1/2"

Elevation

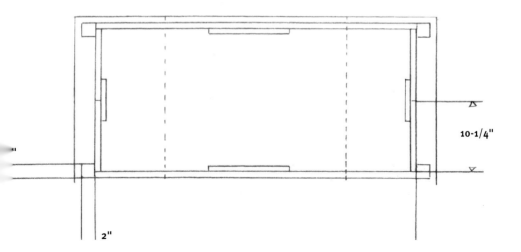

10-1/4"

2"

Plan, section view

nism, but to copy it you would have to do some metalwork.

So I opted for a simpler mechanism used on other portable tables and chairs: wooden cleats. The underside of the desktop has four wooden cleats screwed to the underside that keep the base in its open, rectangular shape.

The cleats are slightly tapered on their outside edges so they slip easily inside the table aprons. It all sounds more complicated than it really is. If you read the rest of this chapter and study the photos, I think you'll see how simple the mechanism really is.

About the Materials

While there is always some flexibility in the materials you use for a project, there are a couple cautions here.

This is not your typical table base. In a typical apron table, you have eight tenons keeping the base rigid, plus some sort of mechanical lock between the top and base, which stiffens everything.

This folding table base has only four tenons. And the only thing holding the top and base together is gravity. So you need to be careful.

The four tenons need to be robust and well-fitted. The aprons are made from 7/8"-thick material so that you can use thicker tenons – 3/8"-thick bareface tenons to be exact. Bareface tenons (which are missing their rear face shoulder) allow you to beef up your mortise walls.

For this table I used teak (*Tectona grandis*) that was 50 years old, wide and beautiful. Teak is quite strong, but it can be difficult to glue. So unless you have some beautiful wide teak sitting around in your garage, consider another appropriate species, such as mahogany, oak, ash or walnut.

Begin with the Legs

The legs are made from 2" x 2" stock. As with all table legs, you want to do what you can to ensure you have "bastard" grain in all four legs. Bastard grain is where the annular rings run at 45° through each leg. When the rings are at 45°, the legs will appear similar on all four faces.

This concept can be difficult to explain until you make a leg that doesn't have bastard grain. A non-bastard-grain leg typically will have grain that is flat-sawn on two faces and quartersawn grain on the other two faces.

These two types of faces reflect light differently and are quite visually distracting. So aim for bastard grain.

The other thing to consider when cutting out your legs is to look for wood where the grain runs vertically through the entire leg. Angled grain can look very distracting, so it pays to cut your legs so that the grain is perfectly vertical.

Legs can be quite wasteful of thick material. Don't be afraid to do some radical surgery. That's the price of good-looking legs.

Fig. 9.4 The right mortise. Here are the four mortises in the legs. As you can see from the apron sitting on top of the leg, the tenon will need only three shoulders instead of four. Shifting the tenon to the back of the apron gives you a thicker mortise wall.

Fig. 9.5 Safer taper. Most table saw tapering jigs put your hands in harm's way. Tapering legs on the jointer can push small machines to their limits. So I like to cut the taper with a band saw and clean the cut with a handplane.

After the leg blanks are roughed out, you can cut the four mortises. The mortises should be 3/8" wide, 1-1/2" deep and about 2-7/8" long. The deep and wide mortises add extra strength to the table base. The length of the mortises allow you a 3/8" edge shoulder at the top of each leg and a 1/4" edge shoulder at the bottom of each tenon.

You have a little flexibility with this joint, but not much.

The 3/8" mortises should be set back 1/2" from the outside face of each leg. This position will allow you to use bareface tenons on the long aprons and result in the front of the apron flush with the outside surface of each leg.

With the mortises cut, you can taper the legs. The taper begins 1" below the apron (or 4-1/2" down from the top of each leg). And the legs taper down to 1" at the floor. These legs taper on only two faces – the two interior faces of the legs. The exterior faces of the legs are left square.

There are lots of ways to taper legs. I cut the taper on a band saw and clean the cuts up with a handplane, a method that is safe and results in a ready-to-finish surface.

Cut the Tenons

The size of the tenons should match the mortises, of course. In this case, the tenons should be 3/8" thick, 2-7/8" wide and 1-1/2" long. The odd thing is that the tenon is not centered on the thickness of the apron. Instead, its inside cheek is actually the inside surface of the apron.

This "bareface" tenon is simpler to cut – one less shoulder. It is easier to fit – there is one less shoulder to trim. And it is stronger because the tenon is thicker. The downside is that your mortise wall might show on the interior of the table base. But that is no big deal – you will hardly (if ever) see it.

Cut the tenons then fit them so they are snug in the mortises. You should have to drive them with firm hand pressure and perhaps a little malleting at the end. If the tenons drop into the mortises like throwing a hot dog down a hallway, then you need to thicken up your tenons by gluing on some veneer or other scraps to the tenon cheeks.

This is an important joint; don't skimp.

I considered drawboring this joint to add some mechanical strength. But the original example I studied didn't have any pegs through the tenon, so I decided to make mine the same. If you aren't as concerned about historical accuracy, drawbore these joints.

Small Apron Relief

On the original table, there is a small cutout on the underside of the long aprons. This small cutout lightens the table – visually and in reality – without reducing the strength of the tenons.

Fig. 9.6 Bareface on the back. Here you can see how there is no face cheek on the inside surface of the apron.

I cut this relief using the band saw. Then I cut the 1/2"-radius curve at the ends of the relief with a saw and rasp. Finally, I trued up all the surfaces with a block plane and sandpaper.

This decorative detail is easy and quick to make. Don't skip it (or your table will look like it was built for the Shaker Army. And that's just weird).

Fig. 9.7 Quick relief. The 1/2"-wide relief on each apron is easy to cut on the band saw. Be sure to make a couple relief cuts so you don't cut yourself into a corner.

Fig. 9.8 Plane together. Clamp the aprons together to true the surfaces of the relief cuts. This is faster, and it ensures the aprons will look alike.

Fig. 9.9 Epoxy time. I used epoxy for this joint because I have found it to be unassailable. It fills gaps. It bonds almost anything. Yeah, it stinks and you have to mix it up, but it is hard to argue with its results.

Glue Up

Gluing the two legs to an apron is a simple job, but if you are using teak (or another difficult-to-glue wood), here is some quick advice:

- The joints should all fit tight-ish (enough said).
- Use glue intended for difficult woods, such as epoxy or polyurethane glue.
- Wipe any oil off the surface of the joints using acetone or (if you don't have acetone) lacquer thinner.
- Clamp the joints and leave them overnight.

The Folding Aprons

The side aprons of the table fold inward to collapse the base to a fairly flat state. The mechanism is surprisingly simple – just six butt hinges installed on the six components of the table's base.

All the hinges in this project are 3" x 1-11/16" butt hinges that use No. 8 screws. The entire project requires five pairs of hinges.

A couple notes: The four side apron pieces need to be the exact same length or the base will not fold completely flat. The closer the pieces are to exactly the same

Fig. 9.10 Punch it. When you have lots of hinges to install, a center punch is quite handy. I think this tool is superior to a hinge-installation bit because the point never breaks.

length, the flatter the base will fold. So as you crosscut your side aprons to final size, I recommend you shoot the ends of any that are a tad too long.

And one more thing: The ends of the apron pieces should all be exactly 90° to the long edges and faces of the boards. Slight changes in angles will wreak bad trouble on your base. So shoot straight and 90°.

To assemble the side aprons, begin by installing the hinge in the middle of the two aprons. With this hinge, the barrel should face the outside of the table's base. On the original, the leaves of the hinge were recessed into mortises on the ends of the two apron pieces.

These recesses are a pain to cut or chop by hand because they are all end grain. I cut them on the table saw (to see a photo of this, skip ahead to the part about installing the hinges in the top pieces).

After cutting the hinge mortises, screw the hinge to the aprons with No. 8 x 1" screws. Because you are screwing into end grain, don't over-tighten the screws or they will lose their grip.

With the center hinge installed, you can install the hinges that attach the fold-

Fig. 9.11 Slotted screws. The appropriate fastener for a piece of furniture from the early 19th century is a slotted brass screw. Modern fasteners (Phillips, Torx, drywall etc.) look wrong.

Fig. 9.12 Three-way fold. With three hinges installed on each end apron, you are ready to attach these flexible aprons to the fixed front and rear aprons.

Fig. 9.13 Easy installation. Push the folding apron into this position. Punch in your screw centers. Drill your pilots. Screw. Done.

ing apron to the front and rear aprons. This is done using butt hinges and No. 8 x 3/4" screws. These are easy to install because they don't require a hinge mortise and all the screws are biting into face grain.

Install a hinge at each end of the folding apron. The hinge's leaf should be attached to the inside face of the folding apron as shown in the photos.

Attaching the folding aprons to the rest of the table is easy. Simply put the front of the folding apron against the inside of the leg and screw the leaf to the inside of the fixed apron. No hinge mortise is necessary.

Once you get the folding aprons installed on one of the fixed aprons, it's easier to install the other fixed apron with all the parts on the floor or an assembly bench. Other than that small detail, the installation process is the same for the other ends of the folding aprons.

Fig. 9.14 On the floor. Install the second fixed apron with the parts on the floor, upside-down.

Fig. 9.15 Simple but clever. When the folding apron is connected to the fixed apron, this is what the inside of the table apron should look like.

Fig. 9.16 Notches for hinges. Here a leaf is up on end on the top of the table saw. I have a 5/8" dado blade installed in the saw and its height matches the thickness of the hinge leaf. Mark where your hinge starts and stops. Nibble out the wood between the two lines.

The Folding Top

As I mentioned at the beginning of this chapter, the top is odd because the barrels of the hinges protrude above the desktop. They actually aren't as annoying as they first appear. Still, if they offend you, look for card-table hinges as an alternative. They are installed on the long edges of the top pieces. (Be aware that if you go this route you will have to change the profile on the edges.)

The top is made of three pieces. The two smaller leaves fold up onto the center piece. By folding up (instead of folding down), the show surface of the desktop is protected when the piece is in storage.

After cutting your three top pieces to their finished sizes, remove the machine marks and cut the recesses for the hinges. As shown in the photo above, I used a table saw with a dado stack. I usually install hinges by hand, but I opted for a machine here because the end grain of this cut is difficult to cut and pare flat.

Install these hinges into their recesses to create the folding top. With the top together, true up the long edges so that everything lines up. This will make it easy to cut the profile on the edges of the desktop.

The profile is, of course, up to you. The original I examined had a bullnose profile all around the desktop. I am quite fond of chamfers, so I planed a 1/4" x 1/4" chamfer on the top and bottom edges of the three desktop pieces.

Fig. 9.17 Odd hinge mortise. Mortising the end grain for hinges is unusual. Use No. 8 x 1" screws and tighten them with care. It's easy to chew up the pilot hole in end grain.

The last bit of construction work on this table is to create the way that the top and base lock together. I opted to make four 3/4" x 3/4" cleats that butt against the four aprons of the base. This simple solution works well.

To make the top easy to install, I beveled one long edge of each cleat. The bevels are 15° and are 1/2" tall. They ends in a 1/2" flat area. The bevels make it easy to drop the top onto the base; the flats lock the desktop to the base.

To install the four cleats, I flipped everything upside down on some sawbenches and centered the base on the underside of the top. Then I screwed the cleats to the underside of the desktop with No. 10 x 1" brass screws.

As you position the cleats, press them firmly against the base, but not too firmly. You don't want to bend the apron at this point. If you do install the cleats too tightly, plane them down with a shoulder plane (or unscrew them and thin them with a block plane).

Clean up all the surfaces, break the edges and prepare the parts for finishing.

I used garnet shellac. I applied three coats, sanding between coats with a #320-grit sanding sponge.

Some Final Thoughts on the Field Desk

I built this field desk so it was fairly close to the original. The only significant change I made was the edge profile around the desktop – and simplifying the attachment mechanism to save you some metalworking.

Fig. 9.18 Helpful bevel. The shallow bevel on the cleats makes it easy to install the desktop on the base.

However, you might consider some changes to the design. Hinging the top with card-table hinges or three-way hinges mortised into the top are both things to strongly consider.

If you are going to use this piece as a desk, consider shortening the legs by 2" or more to get to a more standard 30" desktop height.

One more consideration would be to make the top less than 48" long. The long aprons of this table pushed me out of the range of my 52"-long bar clamps. It wasn't a big deal, but clamping would have been easier with a slightly smaller table (as would have been my material yield from the rough lumber).

Fig. 10.1. A collapsible bookshelf
modeled after a teak original.

12.ᵗʰ Return Ramrods.

CHAPTER 10
COLLAPSIBLE BOOKSHELVES

Bookshelves that fold flat or disassemble are common items among surviving pieces of campaign furniture. These ingenious units were generally pretty small. After all, it's not as if you were traveling overseas with a Carnegie library, and books of the 19th century were usually compact items.

How small? A typical campaign shelf unit is 3' wide, 2' high and 8" to 10" deep. That's not a lot of shelf space.

Many of these shelving units were designed to sit on top of another piece of furniture, such as a campaign chest or desktop. Or they were intended to hang on the wall, which was especially handy during a sea voyage.

Common Types of Portable Shelves

The most common type of portable shelf isn't one you'd expect to see in a book on woodworking because it's mostly metal. These shelves are tubular metal uprights that screw together with two, or usually three, wooden shelves between.

These shelves look spindly but are robust enough for the job.

A less-common variant on these shelves replaces the metal with wooden uprights – usually turned spindles – that screw together with the wooden shelves to produce the finished piece.

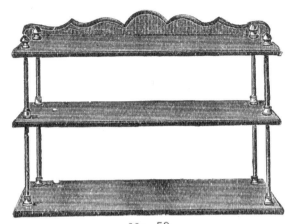

No. 50.
Portable bookshelves with brass standards,
mahogany, oak, teak, or walnut.
2 ft. 8 in. long, 8 in. wide, 22 in. high ... 25/9
2 ft. 11 in. long, 8 in. wide, 22 in. high ... 27/0
No. 51.

Figs. 10.2 & 10.3 Screwed together. The metal uprights screw together with the shelves to produce a fairly sturdy set of shelves.

Another type of shelving unit is a folding book rack. The simplest form of book rack has a flat shelf with two "bookends" that fold flat while traveling. These simple racks are not exclusive to the campaign style; you'll find variants during every furniture period where books were common.

The ends of the three boards are mitered and hinged. Sometimes the ends have handles so you can lift and move the loaded rack.

There are more complex mechanical book racks that also expand in length as well as having folding ends. These usually require some tricky hardware to make them function well, so I decided not to build one for this book.

The third common type of collapsible shelving unit folds like an accordion. You usually remove a center shelf (or two), and the uprights fold in on themselves, turning your shelf unit into a flat pile of lumber. The first time you see it in action, it's actually a little bewildering. But it is quite cool.

This type of shelf unit requires no special hardware – just a small pile of butt hinges. And there is almost no real joinery to speak of. So it's an ideal project for the woodworker without access to a forge or a metal shop.

These accordion-style shelves came in several different sizes and configurations that were embellished or plain. Some versions were designed to hang on a wall; others sat on top of a chest or desk.

The shelves I built for this book are based on a unit I admired in one of the Christopher Clarke Antiques catalogs. The original was made from teak; mine is

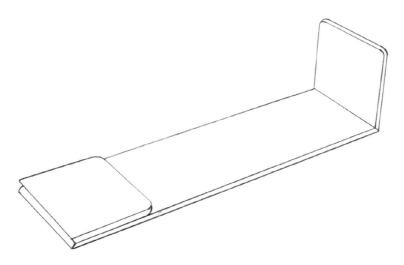

Fig. 10.4 Three boards. This simple folding book rack is about 28" wide. The folding ends are each 6" long. All three pieces are about 8-1/2" wide.

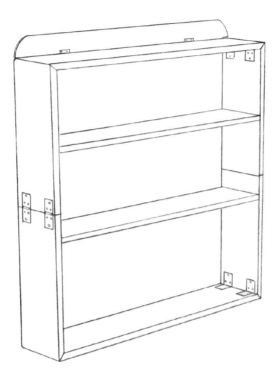

Fig. 10.5 For hanging. These large folding shelves were designed to hang on the wall. Note that the barrels of the hinges on the uprights are equidistant from both the top and bottom of the case. This detail allows the unit to fold flat.

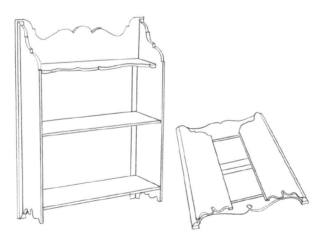

Fig. 10.6 More modern. These folding shelves work like shelves you can find at the department store. The three shelves fold up, which allows the ends to fold in, making a single flat panel.

Fig. 10.7 The original. This is the original version of these shelves in teak. I altered the top profile slightly, but otherwise mine is quite similar. (Courtesy of Christopher Clarke Antiques)

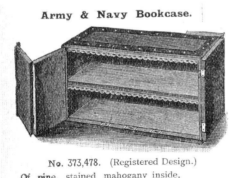

Army & Navy Bookcase.

No. 373,478. (Registered Design.)

Of pine, stained mahogany inside, outside painted and iron bound, size, 30 in. long, 7 in. wide, 19 in. high £2 0 3

This can be made of any size to order.

Fig. 10.8 Folding front. The Army & Navy Bookcase is made of pine. It is painted on the outside but stained to look like mahogany on the inside. The corners are bound in iron. Most interesting is how the folding doors actually fold back around the case, keeping them out of the way. Dimensions: 30" W x 19" H x 7" D.

mahogany. While the only joinery in the whole project is cutting two dados, you will become quite an expert at installing butt hinges. It takes 12 hinges to get the whole thing to work. And installing the hinges precisely makes the shelf unit sturdier and makes it collapse more smoothly.

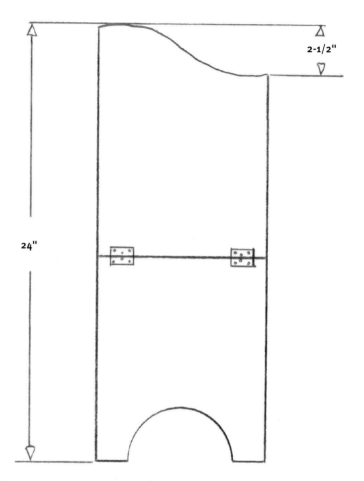

Profile

❧ COLLAPSIBLE SHELVES ❧

NO.	PART	SIZES (INCHES)		
		T	W	L
2	Uprights	7/8	9-1/2	24-1/8
2	Hinged shelves	3/4	9-1/2	20-5/8
1	Removable shelf	3/4	9-1/2	21-3/8
1	Dropped edge	3/4	2	20-5/8

Dimensions on drawing: 2-1/2", 24"

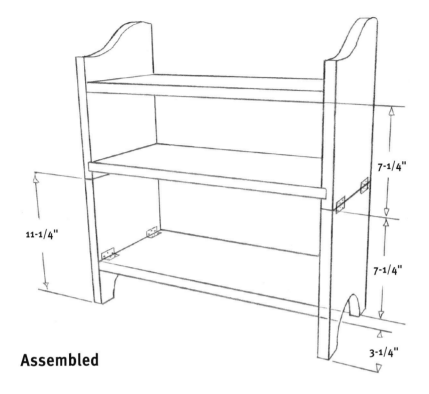

Assembled

Begin With the Uprights

The two ends of the unit – called the uprights – look best if made from a board that is the full 9-1/2" width and has the grain's cathedral running up its middle. If wood is scarce, the shelves can be made from narrower boards that are glued up the final width. The shelves are usually covered by books, so they don't show.

Cut the uprights to 24-1/8" long. The extra 1/8" is for the kerf when separating the top from the bottom. Before making this critical crosscut, mark the uprights with a cabinetmaker's triangle so you can easily distinguish how the pieces should be reassembled with hinges.

Then crosscut the uprights at 11-1/4" up from the base.

Before installing the hinges, cut the decorative shapes at the top and bottom of the uprights. The base is half of a circle with a 3" radius. The top is a simple ogee that is 2-1/2" tall and switches from concave to convex on the center of the width of the upright.

Now is the best time to remove any machine marks from the uprights. You'll find that planing or sanding the boards after installing the hinges is a bad idea – it can make the mechanism sloppy.

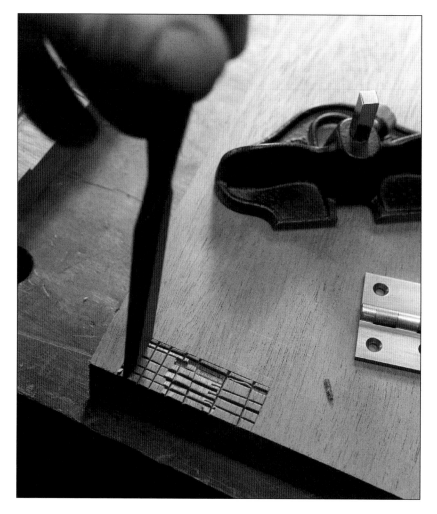

Fig. 10.9 Chop & rout. To cut a hinge mortise, first chop across the grain deeply. Then chop parallel to the grain more shallowly to avoid splitting the work. Pop out the waste with a router plane.

First Install

When you hinge the two pieces of the upright together, you want zero gap between the top and bottom piece. Lay out the location of the hinge mortises with care. Mine are set in 1/2" from the long edges of the uprights. And before you cut the mortises, clamp the top and bottom of the upright together and show the hinge to your layout lines. They should match.

Chop out the mortises and clean up the bottom of each mortise with a router plane. The depth of these mortises should be the exact thickness of the hinge's leaf.

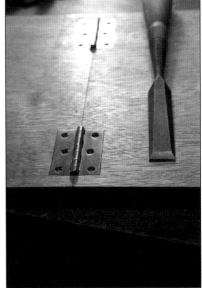

Fig. 10.10 Punch it. Clamp the top and bottom together to ensure the parts are aligned and stay that way as you install the hinges. I use a center punch to mark where the screw holes should go.

Fig. 10.11 Go for gold. The better the fit, the better the mechanism will work. Plus, unlike with most hinges, these are visible from the outside of the piece.

I install hinges with the assistance of a center punch and a birdcage awl. Punch in at each hole in the hinge leaf. Drill your pilot hole. Follow that up with a few twists of the awl. This three-step process makes a nice tapered hole for the screws.

When installing a lot of brass screws, I make life easier by cutting the threads in my pilot holes with a steel screw that is identical to my brass ones. I'll drive the steel screw into each hole with an electric drill/driver. Then retract it. This makes it simple to install the brass screws without chewing up their slots.

With the hinges installed on both uprights, determine a good location for the dado that will hold the sliding shelf. The dado has to miss the screws from your hinges and be in a place that will fit your books both above and below the removable shelf. My dado is located 3/4" up from the bottom edge of the top upright.

Remove the hinges and cut the 3/4"-wide x 3/8"-deep dado on both uprights.

Hinge the Shelves

The next step is to install the hinges on the shelves. Install hinges on the underside of the top shelf and the top surface of the lowest shelf. These hinge mortises are also set 1/2" in from the long edges of the shelves and the depth of the mortises is the same as the thickness of the hinge leaf.

Fig. 10.12 Not in the way. This 3/4"-wide x 3/8"-deep dado is placed in a spot where it won't interfere with my hinges' screws.

Install all eight hinges before attempting to attach anything to the uprights.

The next part is where you need to be careful. If you make a mistake the shelves will not fold flat. Here's the important fact to remember: The hinge barrels of the top and bottom shelves need to be equidistant from the hinge barrels in the uprights.

On this unit, that magic distance is 7-1/4".

Put another way, the top surface of the bottom shelf needs to be 7-1/4" from the hinge barrels in the uprights. And the bottom surface of the top shelf needs to be 7-1/4" from the hinge barrels in the uprights.

As much as I dislike measuring, this is one place where it's difficult to avoid. Lay out the location of the hinge mortises on the uprights for the bottom shelf only. Then do something that could very well save your bacon: Place the parts on your bench in a pseudo dry-fit and check your layout a few times.

The hinge mortises in the uprights are different than the mortises everywhere else in this project. For one, they are larger because they have to hold both the leaf and the barrel of each hinge. Second, they need to be deeper than the thickness of the hinge leaf.

If you make these mortises too shallow, the finished unit will wobble. If you make the mortises too deep, the hinge will bind and nothing will open or close.

How deep should each hinge mortise be? The thickness of the hinge plus half

Fig. 10.13 An odd dry-fit. After laying out the location of the mortises on the uprights, I am showing the bottom shelf to the uprights.

of the complete hinge barrel (that's both the knuckle and the pin). On your first mortise, my advice is to sneak up on the perfect depth. When you find the proper depth, the shelves will stop at a perfect 90° to the upright.

Then lock in that depth on your router plane and don't change it until you are done mortising.

Screw the bottom shelf in place. The uprights should fold flat against the bottom shelf. With the unit all folded up, you can use the layout marks to put the upper shelf in the correct spot without any real measuring.

Make the four mortises for the top shelf and screw everything together. The unit should fold completely flat. If it won't fold flat, your mortises are in the wrong place.

The Middle Shelf

Cut the middle shelf to its finished length and plane it until it fits snug but slides smoothly into its dado. To increase the stability of the unit, I added a 2"-wide "dropped edge" to the underside of the shelf. Usually a "dropped" edge acts like a brace to keep a shelf from sagging. In this case it helps stabilize the carcase.

I cut the dropped edge to a too-tight fit between the uprights and used a shooting board and a plane to get it to fit just right. Then I glued it to the underside of the middle shelf while the middle shelf was in place between the uprights.

Fig. 10.14 Deeper mortises. To ensure the stability of the finished unit, these mortises need to be a little deeper so the shelf will stop at 90° to the uprights.

Fig. 10.15 Here's the trick. Carry the location of the hinge mortise for the lower shelf onto the edge. Then carry that line over to the other upright (which is folded against it). Pull that line down and you have made the most critical layout line for the next set of hinge mortises.

Fig. 10.16 Glued in place. Adding the dropped edge while the case is assembled removes the risk of it sliding around as you apply clamp pressure.

Finishing the Bookshelves

Take the shelves apart and clean up any tool marks you missed before. Remember: The less material you remove the sturdier the shelves will be. Break the boards' sharp edges with sandpaper or a plane.

This project has a simple finishing schedule: two coats of garnet shellac followed by a coat of black wax. The shellac colors the mahogany a nice dark honey. The black wax gets lodged in the pores and ensures the other people on your voyage to India won't think you a "griffin" out on your first tour.

Fig. 11.1. A traveling bookcase
in quartered oak.

13th Shoulder Firelock.

CHAPTER 11
TRAVELING BOOKCASE

Folding clamshell bookcases weren't just for officers or bureaucrats of the British Empire. These tough pieces of cabinetwork were ideal for students or any bibliophile who had to be mobile.

Built like a chest or trunk, these bookcases were typically dovetailed at the corners for maximum strength. The interiors varied. They all had shelves – of course. Sometimes the shelves were adjustable; sometimes they were fixed. You might find cubbyholes or drawers near the base of the chest.

And sometimes each side of the bookcase was further protected by a hinged door that was solid wood, glass or a metal mesh.

All of the examples I've encountered were secured with a chest lock or a hasp. The bookcases also wore brass or iron corner guards to protect the books if the piece took a serious hit.

The example I've built for this book is pretty simple. It's made from quarter-sawn oak and is dovetailed at the corners with half-blind dovetails. Each half of the clamshell case features two adjustable shelves that are suited to hold smaller books. At the base of the carcase are four dovetailed drawers that are fronted by flush drawer pulls.

The backs of the carcase are panels that float in grooves in the carcase

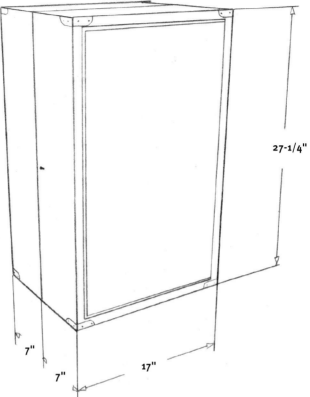

27-1/4"

7"

7"

17"

Exterior

NO.	PART	SIZES (INCHES)		
		T	W	L
4	Tops & bottoms	3/4	7	16-3/4
4	Sides	3/4	7	27-1/4
2	Backs	5/8	15-3/4	26
6	Shelves	1/2	6-1/4	15-7/8
2	Vertical dividers	1/2	6-1/4	3-3/4
4	Drawer fronts	5/8	3-3/8	7-1/2

∿ TRAVELING BOOKCASE ∿

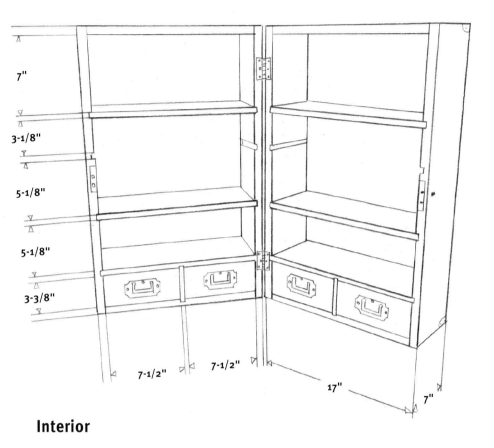

7"

3-1/8"

5-1/8"

5-1/8"

3-3/8"

7-1/2"

7-1/2"

17"

7"

Interior

pieces. In this piece, I've covered the interior with an embossed wallpaper. Then I painted and shellacked the paper to make it look vintage. The exterior is finished with garnet shellac.

Build the Carcase

The carcase of this bookcase is somewhat like a dovetailed drawer. All the corners are joined by half-blind dovetails. The backs float in grooves in the dovetailed shells. Begin construction by dovetailing the tops and bottoms to the sides of the carcase.

To match many bookcases of the period, I cut the tails on the tops and bottoms of the carcases. The pins are on the sides. Because these bookcases normally sit on top of another piece (such as a campaign chest), the orientation of the pins and tails isn't much of an issue.

After cutting the tails and pins, plow the 1/4" x 1/4" grooves for the carcase backs. The grooves are 1/4" from the outside edge of the carcase. Then lay out the

Fig. 11.2 Don't measure. Strike one wall of each dado for the shelves. Then use the shelf material to strike the other line of the dado. This ensures a good fit.

Fig. 11.3 Saw the walls. Place your thumb in the groove to stop your saw as you saw each wall of the dado.

Fig. 11.4 Choppy. Break up the waste between the dado walls with a chisel that is the same width as the dado.

Fig. 11.5 Plow the waste. Remove most of the waste with a chisel. Work bevel-up to remove material quickly; work bevel-down to add some control.

locations of the 1/2"-wide x 1/4"-deep dados for the shelves. I gang the carcase parts together to make the layout (relatively) foolproof.

Saw out the walls of the dados, then chop up the waste with a 1/2"-wide chisel. Plow the waste out with the chisel. Try working both bevel-up and bevel-down. The bevel-up orientation will remove waste in a hurry – perhaps to the point where you will go below your desired depth. Chiseling bevel-down is slower, but you don't take as big a bite. I usually remove most of the waste with the chisel bevel-up, then I finish up with it bevel-down.

After you have the bottom of your dado roughed out, clean it up to a consistent depth with a router plane. You also can use the side of the router plane's iron to scrape the vertical walls of the dado, fairing and squaring them.

With the dados cut, knock the carcases together and measure the final dimensions of the back pieces. Cut the back panels to size, then rabbet all four edges so the panel floats in the grooves. Be sure to leave some space for expansion of the back. I used quartersawn oak, which doesn't move much, so I allowed for only 1/8" of movement in each panel.

Gluing up the carcases is an odd job. You want to glue each carcase so its joints are tight. But you also want to glue up each carcase so it is the same shape

Fig. 11.6 Plunge forward. The router plane isn't suited to take a big bite. The waste jams up against the post of the iron too easily. Use the router to remove the smallest amount of waste from the bottom of the dado.

Fig. 11.7 About that much. I don't cut my panels to size until I have the carcases dry-fit. This (usually) prevents me from making a stupid error.

Fig. 11.8 Rabbet that. Cut the rabbets on the back panels. Cut the rabbets across the grain first. Then follow that with the rabbets that run parallel to the grain.

as its mate. Otherwise, you will end up (I promise) with two carcases that are different shapes.

So apply glue, then clamp up each carcase independently. Place the two assemblies on top of one another and clamp them together along the seam. Once those clamps are on, check the uber-assembly for squareness. After the glue is dry, plane up the carcases individually. Then clamp them together and fair the seam between the two shells.

Install the Lock

This is an excellent time to install the hinges and lock. While most woodworkers have installed butt hinges, many have not installed a chest lock. They are actually simple to install if you take the process one step at a time and don't measure too much.

The key to installing a chest lock is to drill a hole where the pin will go. The pin is the most important part of the lock. The key is inserted onto the pin then rotates on it to unlock the bookcase. So all the layout is determined from the pin.

Measure (shudder) from the top of the lock to the center of the pin. Transfer that measurement to the carcase and make a dimple with an awl. You want to drill at this location a hole through the carcase that is slightly smaller than the diameter of the pin itself (1/64" or 1/32" undersized is about right).

Fig. 11.9 Glue the two. You want these carcases to mate. So glue them up in tandem. Clamp the tops, bottoms and sides. But also clamp the carcases together so their edges align.

Fig. 11.10 On a platform. A leg vise and a platform (made from scrap) is a powerful setup for planing the joints of your carcases.

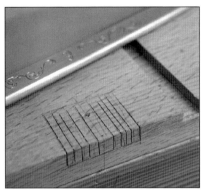

Fig. 11.12 The bulk of the waste. Saw-cuts help break up the waste. Chop parallel to the grain lines with a chisel to remove most of the waste.

Fig. 11.11 One hole. A scant hole in the carcase guides the installation of the chest lock.

Fig. 11.13 Use the hole. The hole you bored for the pin also guides the installation of the escutcheon. Trace around the escutcheon with a fine pencil.

Fig. 11.14 Saw out the waste. Saw the walls of the hole for the escutcheon, then chisel out any waste.

Fig. 11.15 The final recess. Press the lock back into place and trace around its exterior plate. Chop out the waste.

Then, from the inside of the carcase, press the lock into the hole. It should stick there.

With the lock pressed into the hole you can trace around its inside case with a thick (or blunt) pencil. This pencil line represents the next recess you should saw and chop out. Then you can install the press-in escutcheon on the outside of the carcase.

Interior Structures

These bookcases can be divided up in a variety of ways. This one has two drawers at the bottom of each case. When I started on this case, my plan was to have only one shelf on each side. After assembling the carcase, I decided to add a couple more shelves and make them adjustable. This was an easy matter of sawing some more dados in the carcase walls.

At this point I also had to saw the 1/2" x 1/8" dados for the dividers between the drawers in each carcase. This was a simple matter of sawing, chiseling and routing the waste. You can then glue these pieces into the carcase.

Then I turned my attention to the drawers. Despite my best efforts, the holes for the drawers were all slightly different. So I fit individually the drawer parts for each drawer opening. When I do this sort of work, I fit the drawer front so it will just sneak into its opening all around. I cut the drawer back to that same length.

Fig. 11.16 Line up the dados. I cut the dados for the drawer dividers after assembly. Using a square, I lined up the walls of the dados and marked out what needed to be cut away.

I fit the drawer sides so they slide in and out of the carcase like I want the finished drawer to slide. I wait to cut the drawer bottom until the drawer is assembled.

The drawers I make are typical for the 18th and 19th centuries. The sides join the drawer back with through-dovetails. The sides join the drawer front with half-blind (the British call them "lap") dovetails. The bottom slides into the assembled drawer in a groove plowed into the sides and drawer front.

Once the joints are cut, glue up the drawers. Make sure the drawers are dead square – you can pull them into square with a tight and well-fit drawer bottom if necessary.

Once your drawers are assembled, clean up the joints with a plane and fit each drawer into its opening. The tighter the fit, the less likely the drawer will bind when you pull it out.

Then add the pulls. I used some vintage pulls that were made in the mid-20th century, which are surprisingly similar to ones made today. Just as when you installed the lock, installing the pulls is a multi-stage process. First you waste away the deepest and smallest recess for the pull. Then you fit the pull into that hole and trace around the backplate. Then mortise out the area for the backplate and you can screw the pull in place.

Don't be afraid to file parts of the pull to make it fit or function.

Fig. 11.17 Parts in place. Fit your drawer parts so they match the dimensions of the drawer opening. If the individual parts fit too tight, the drawer will surely stick.

Fig. 11.18 Drilled out. I usually remove most of the waste with a drill – in this case a Forstner bit. All this ugliness will be hidden behind the pull's backplate.

Fig. 11.19 Traced & chopped. After fitting the pull into the first recess, press it down and trace around the backplate. Then you can chop out that waste.

Finish the Interior

Some of these bookcases were lined with felt, cloth or some sort of wallpaper. To give this bookcase a Victorian look, I lined the interior with an embossed wallpaper. Then I painted the wallpaper and coated it with shellac (like the rest of the carcase).

Adding wallpaper is easy. Cut the paper so it fits the opening (or is slightly bigger that the space required). Roll some wallpaper paste on the back of the wallpaper. Fold the pasted surfaces on themselves, closing them like a book. Wait 10 minutes.

Then you can unfold the wallpaper and apply it to the wood. Use a wallpaper brush to press the paper to the wood. Don't use a squeegee tool if you are using embossed wallpaper – it will destroy the pattern.

If your paper is oversized, trim it into the corner with a utility knife. Then turn your attention to the next piece of wallpaper. Let the paste dry for 24 hours before trimming the bits that cover the dados.

Paint the wallpaper if you like; I used a green milk paint I had on hand. With embossed wallpaper you can create a nice two-tone effect with little

Fig. 11.20 Easy wallpapering. If you've ever hung wallpaper, you'll be amazed how easy it is to do on a horizontal surface. It doesn't sag.

effort. Brush on a coat of paint. Wait about five minutes for the paint to set up a bit. Then gently wipe the paper with a sponge. The sponge will remove the paint from the high spots.

You can use contrasting colors to paint the high spots and low spots. But remember: Books will cover the wallpaper most of the time. So don't go too crazy.

After the paint dries, finish the entire case. I wanted the outside to look a bit aged, though not distressed. So I finished the entire case, inside and out, with two coats of garnet shellac. Then I wiped a black wax on to the exterior surfaces of the carcase. After the wax flashed, I wiped off the excess, leaving the black in the pores.

Then I coated the entire piece, inside and out, with one coat of a dull lacquer to cut back some of the shine from the shellac.

The final step was to add some corner hardware. As an experiment, I used applied corner guards that are secured with escutcheon pins. They don't look as nice as inset corner guards, but they are better than nothing.

Fig. 11.21 Paste then trim. Use one piece of paper on the sides of the carcase. After the paste has dried 24 hours, use a knife to slice away the paper covering the dados.

Fig. 11.22 A little dab. After the paint flashes, gently wipe the high spots with a sponge to brush away part of the paint.

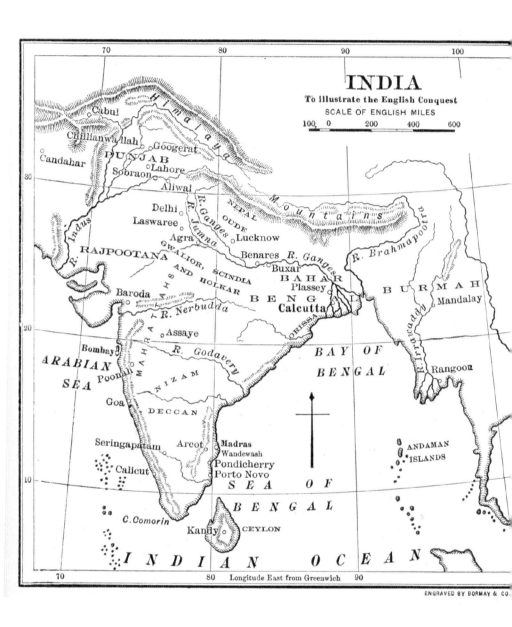

FIG. 2. A map of England's holdings in India from "A Short History of England" by Katharine Coman and Elizabeth Kendall (1922).

14ᵗʰ Rest Firelock.

AFTERWORD
ON WAR & REGRETS

Building a piece of campaign furniture is no more a celebration of war than driving a Volkswagen is a celebration of the Third Reich.

The plain fact of the matter is that conquest and defense are rich sources of innovation, improvisation and technological advances. The molded plywood of Charles and Ray Eames was used by the Navy in World War II for splints and stretchers. That knowledge was turned to making molded plywood furniture, including the iconic Eames chair.

The needs of the British Empire and its far-flung colonies created a style of furniture that was rugged, beautiful and stripped of ornament. There is little doubt in my mind that the utilitarian and plain aspects of campaign furniture represent the roots of Danish modern, Bauhaus and other 20th-century design trends.

So I do not regret the 28 months I spent researching, building and writing this book. I think the campaign furniture style is one of the most important and overlooked furniture movements of the last 200 years.

But I do have regrets.

When I set out to build the projects for this book, I consciously set aside my aversion to exotic tropical hardwoods. When I write about an historical style, I immerse myself in it as much as possible so I can understand it from the inside.

THE DEATH OF PURSOOT—A TALE OF TIGER-HUNTING.— SEE PAGE 14.

That means ignoring well-known rules about wood movement, technological advances in adhesives and (in this case) deforestation.

When I reject my modern prejudices I usually find gold. I think the past has a lot to teach us. Time and again, I've found that old ways of woodworking are usually smarter, more nuanced and more practical than our own.

But when it comes to selecting wood for a project, I'm not so sure. Most pieces of campaign furniture were built using mahogany, camphor, teak, padauk, oak or walnut. The exotics on this list were beyond plentiful in the 18th and 19th centuries. (Imagine teak being cheaper than red oak.) The supply at the time seemed almost limitless according to the accounts of the day.

I know that we furniture makers are not the primary offenders when it comes to stripping the land of tropical hardwoods. But I also know that writing a book featuring tropical hardwoods is no small affair.

So as you are picking out the wood for your first (or next) piece of campaign furniture, consider this: walnut. American and European walnut were a common staple of the campaign furniture trade, so they are an appropriate choice.

Here in the Ohio River valley, we have so much walnut that we used it to frame houses and make sash. Heck, I have a pile of walnut in my shop that is bigger than a car.

If you choose to use mahogany or another exotic, consider looking for recycled lumber. Some of the wood in this book came from a (trashed) recycled dining set I purchased from a woodworker who finally decided to lay down his tools.

That old and recycled mahogany was darker, finer and more beautiful than any modern stick of mahogany I have laid my hands on. So finding recycled wood can actually improve your finished piece (as opposed to using recyled McDLT boxes to make a Trex garden bench).

In the end, it is your choice. I encourage you to ignore every word I have just written and do your own research to make an informed decision.

I don't want blinded readers any more than I want to spend a single day living in a totalitarian regime. You are free to make a choice about what you build, how you build it and what materials you use to build. So make it.

— Christopher Schwarz

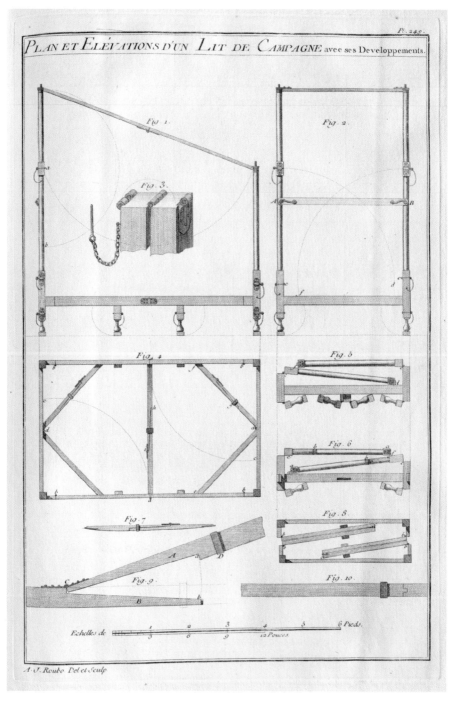

FIG. 3. Plate 249 from "l'Art du Menuisier."

15th Order Firelock.

APPENDIX A
ROUBO ON CAMPAIGNING

L ike many woodworking writers of the 18th century, André-Jacob Roubo included a section in "l'Art du Menuisier" on campaign furniture.
As far I know, this section has not been translated into English.

I asked Michele P. Pagan, who translated sections of Roubo on marquetry,
finishing and furniture-making, to tackle the short section on campaign furniture. She agreed immediately. What follows is a translation of Roubo's text that
discusses three plates in his books: 249, 250 and 251. Note: Parts of the text that
are in parentheses are Roubo's words in translation. Text that is in brackets
has been added by the editors or the translator. The French word for "inch" is
translated as "thumb" in this text. A "line" is one-twelfth of a thumb.

Section III: Description of Campaign Beds, etc.

Description of different Types of Campaign Beds, Their Shapes and Construction

Plate 249: Plan and Elevations of a Campaign Bed with Its Illustrations:

The beds of which I just made the description are called "Brigantines" and are hardly used except in war or in voyages of the grand masters, who, having a numerous following, cannot find en route the number of beds sufficient for them and their people.

Two things are to be considered in the construction of these beds, namely, their lightness and convenience, because being subject to being transported often, it is necessary that they be very light, and that they take the least space possible. This has caused us to invent different ways of folding or breaking them (in workman's terms). That which is represented in this plate, although costly and very complicated, is the best, and one of the most solid that we make use of.

This bed, such as is represented in figures 1 and 2, which represents the elevation of the side and the end, and figure 4, which represents the [plan view], breaks as much in height as in its width, namely, the legs at the back, figure 1, at point "*a.*" The height of the leg folds from "*a*" to "*b,*" which I have indicated by a punctuated semi-circle.

After this break, the legs, like those of the front, break from within, namely, that of the right (or the left, which is equal), figure 2, at point "*e,*" from where it folds on the crosspiece at point "*d,*" and that on the left to point "*e,*" from which it folds on the other leg at point "*f.*" Look at figure 5, which represents these feet thus folded, as well as those below, of which the movement is indicated in the elevations of figure 1 and 2, by punctuated arcs. Look also at figure 6, which represents these same broken legs and viewed from within, so that one can recognize the first break in the legs or columns, which I have marked these same letters as on the elevations, to facilitate the understanding of the discussion.

The framing of this bed breaks in three places, namely in the middle "*a,*" figure 4, and at the two ends "*b-b,*" at about 3 thumbs from their assembly. After having removed the slashes from within, and the crosspiece from the middle, which I will speak of next, you fold the frames to the inside, one to the right and the other to the left, such that they rejoin the crosspieces of the ends at point "*c-c.*" Look at figure 8, which represents this bed thus folded, viewed from above.

Each of the breaks of the legs is finished with two iron hinges, the pin of which is riveted and attached to the two ends of the legs, and the other attached the same on these legs, but the pin of which is mobile, such that it is removed to fold the leg, and is replaced to hold it straight, as you can see in figure 3, where this mobile pin has one eye in its head, to hold a chain which is attached to the leg, for fear that it be lost.

The slats at the ends are joined together by a hinge *"d,"* figure 4. You make them enter at their ends into some mortises made for this effect in the middle of the crosspiece and in the slashes, into which you cannot, however, make them enter except by breaking one of the two slats, which is done in the following manner:

You make in the end of the two pieces *A,B,* figure 9, destined to make a broken slat, two notches *a,b,* on the horizontal, of about one thumb in length, plus a width at the end as that of the base, so as to render the pieces stronger on the side. These two notches should be perfectly equal, so that the body of one piece fills the void of the other. To make the joint of these notches stronger, you make at both ends of each piece small tongues, which prevent them from moving. Then you hold the two pieces together by means of a hinge *C,* placed on its face, such that they can open or close according to your judgment. They subsequently remain closed by means of an iron yoke *D,* which you slide over the joint after closing it, as I have indicated in this figure by punctuations. You can see this in figure 10, which represents the slat viewed on the horizontal, with the iron yoke in its place.

After what I just said, it is really easy to see that after having made the slat enter straight into the frame of the bed at point *e,* figure 4, you make the two ends join together in the crosspiece. Then the break of the other slat being open, you make its tenon enter into the other side, at point *f.* Then you close the break, of which the opening, in shortening the slat, facilitates the entry of the tenon. You make the yoke *g* slide on the join of the break of the slat, which thus becomes as solid as if it were a single piece, and by this means, you hold the frame in place.

The crossbar of the middle of these beds breaks equally in two parts, in the same way as the slats, whether on the level, as that of *h-i,* figure 4, or on edge, as represented in figure 7, which is, I believe the better way.

The breaks, for the crossbar in the middle as with the slats, are not only necessary to hold the frames in place, but also to bind up the canvas which is attached above, which serves as the base of the bed. This same canvas serves also as the back, and it is for this reason attached on a crosspiece *AB,* figure 2, which enters into some pegs placed behind the legs, to which you hold it by means of two hooks.

These beds have hardly any canopy, but only four bars which enter into some studs placed at the ends of the legs, as you can see in figures 1 and 2, where this bar is broken into two parts to take less space when the bed is disassembled.

Because these beds are liable to be set up and dismantled often, the ends of the bars that are the tester, or "tent," are fitted with iron, so that they not be likely to break, like the tenons and crosspieces of the middle of the bed, which we likewise make of iron, so that they last longer, and that the mortises destined to receive them be smaller, which weakens the frame less.

These sorts of beds are very convenient, given that by means of all their breaks, they take up no more space than about 15 thumbs squared, by 2 feet and a half to 3 feet, which is their normal width. Then you can put them into a type of trunk or leather sack destined for this use, which makes them very easy to transport. At the same time, one wouldn't to conceal [or hide away] these beds, since they are well made, close solidly, and cost a lot, given their large number of breaks. What's more, they require a certain amount of time for setting up and dismantling, and you are often likely to lose some pieces, especially in a hurried situation, which a decampment requires, or a completely other occasion where it is almost impossible to forget nothing, and to have even the time to fold these beds.

That's why I believed it necessary to give a model of a campaign bed, which, truthfully, takes a bit more space when it is folded, than that which I just described, but which has the advantage of being very easy to set up and in very little time, and which has the distinction that all the pieces that compose it hold together, and are not consequently likely to be lost.

Plate 250: Different types of Seats and Folding Beds or Campaign Beds

This bed, of which the elevation is represented in figure 9 and the [plan] in figure 11, is composed of four legs or uprights of 4 feet in height, assembled normally with some crosspieces, as the base as well as at the space for the backrest. The two frames which are broken in the middle form two chassis (on which is attached the ticking which serves as the base of the bed), and are held to the legs by means of four hinges, which give them the freedom to move when you judge appropriate. When the bed is folded, the top of the face "a" is joined to the leg at point "b," and that of "c" joins up with the other leg at point "d." The tester of this bed is made of three chassis, all closing with hinges, which [fold] one on the other, as with the two [hinged] at one of the bed ends, and at the other they enter into some studs placed at the end of two other legs, to which they hold with some hooks.

When you dismantle the beds, the chassis *"e-f"* folds down on the legs outside. That of *"g-h"* folds onto the first, and that of *"i-l"* onto the latter. I have indicated this by some punctuated arcs, which indicate the different revolutions of these chassis, which you can see in figure 10, which represents this bed completely folded, and where I put the same letters as in the elevation.

When this bed is set up, you hold it apart by four iron hooks attached to the legs, and you support the joint in the middle of the frames by two iron uprights, which have a square return pierced with a hole at its extremity. This serves to hold the leg or iron upright with the frame, by means of a pin which, passing across this hole, enters into the frame. The crossbars of the middle of this bed should be curved and hollowed, like those of the trestle chassis, so that the canvas, which makes the base of these beds, doesn't hold anything on top when one lays there.

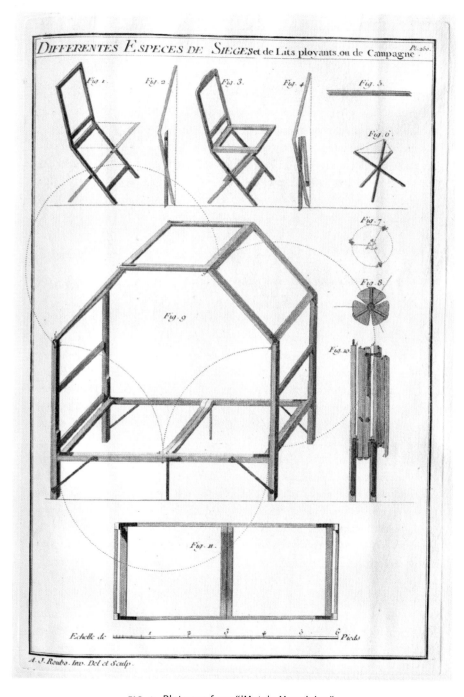

FIG. 4. Plate 250 from "l'Art du Menuisier."

In general, beech serves for the construction of camp beds, and you should choose the very healthy ones, given the little size of the pieces which compose them, which is necessary to make them the lightest weight.

The size of the legs should be from 2 thumbs squared at most, the width of the frames and crossbars, from 2 thumbs to 2 and a half thumbs, by 1 thumb thickness. As to the rest of the pieces, they should be very lightweight.

These beds are not likely to have any type of decoration. It suffices that they be neatly and solidly made. That is all that is necessary.

There is still another type of camp bed, called a Trestle Bed, which is nothing but a type of folding bed, of which the crossbars on top are 6 feet in length, and the legs 3 feet high at most, and 2 feet and a half at the smallest. These legs are assembled by tenon in the crossbars up high, at about 15 thumbs from the end, and receive through the bottom the spacers which hold them apart.

The legs of trestle beds are held together with some screws which pass crosswise, and are held with a nut.

The side of the wood of trestle beds should be from one and a half thumbs squared to 2 thumbs, according to their size. You should note to cut down the interior ridge of the upper crossbar, so that it doesn't cut the straps that are attached above.

Trestle beds are not, properly speaking, camp beds, because they take up too much space, and consequently make a too difficult transport. They are not used at the Court except for the Guards, and in the homes of the Nobles, in their antechambers, and for the beds of their domestics. The owners make use of them when they are obliged to sleep their children or their domestics in spaces which should remain free during the day.

Camp beds that I just spoke of are used by all the general Officers. But when the King, or some other great Prince goes with the Army, they carry beds for them a bit similar to the French Bed with posts, with the exception that the posts are cut into two parts in height, and the crossbars and frames of the bed all come apart in the following way:

You begin by assembling the crossbars, in the front and in the back, by dovetail at the legs, noting that the dovetail not pass across the latter, and that the cutaway of the crossbar enter by about 3 lines into the leg, as you can see in figure 12 and 14 [Plate 251]. This being done, you pierce the hole of the screw (which is normally placed in the frame) across the tail, such that in tightening the screw, you hold the crossbar at the same time, above which you pass the plates *AB*, *CD*, figures 16 and 17, which you extend from there to the notch. You make this enter into the leg so that it doesn't move when tightening the screw. Look at figures 15, 16 and 17, which represent the screw with the plate, viewed from the side and the face.

The base of these beds is filled with straps or canvas attached to the two frames, of which the spread is held in the middle by a crossbar attached to one of the frames by a hinge, and folds up when you dismantle the bed.

The break of the legs is set up with screws, which hold at the shortest end, and enter into a nut placed at the other end. Look at figure 10, which represents the end of a leg with its screw, and that of 11, which represents this same leg in sideview and all set up. You can see the construction of the screw and its nut, which are attached with ferrules that grasp the ends of the legs at the location of the joint. The height of these legs or columns is ended by an ordinary pin, which receives the ends of the chassis of the tester of the bed, which enters into a notch there. The ends are finished with iron, as represented in figure 13. Look at figures 8 and 9, which represent the elevations of the side and face of this bed, which is that which serves the King when he is on a campaign. When it is dismantled, it is held in a leather sack of about 13 to 14 thumbs in diameter, by 6 and a half feet in length.

While I spoke of different types of seats, I made mention of those of the country, of which I reserved the description with that of beds of this type.

The seats that we make the most use of in the country are the folding ones, of which I made the description, with the exception of those of the campaign-style, which are made the simplest and the lightest possible, to make their transport easier. After the folding ones, we have invented types of chairs named "perroquets," which are nothing other than folding ones to which we have added a back. Look at figures 1 and 2 [Plate 250], which represent this chair open and closed.

The back and the top of these chairs are finished with leather, like those of the folding campaign chairs. To make them softer, we have finished them in leather and ordinary horsehair, which requires making a chassis to hold the top of the seat, which is attached at one end with a hinge with the crossbar at the height of the legs in the front, and at the other is pressed on that of the back, as you can see in figure 3. When the seat is folded, this seat falls back in the front. Look at figure 4.

The construction of these sorts of chairs is really simple: Their frames are nothing but straight, uniform wood pieces, of a thumb and a half in width, by one thumb thick. The height of the seat is always the same: there is nothing but their width, which you reduce to 14 or 15 thumbs at most, so that they take up less space.

We make yet another type of small seat without a back, which are a very good invention for taking less place when they are folded. These seats are called "echaudés," and are composed of three uprights of 26 thumbs in length, of a triangular form in their design, such that the three together form a bundle of 2 thumbs diameter. Note that they don't join exactly at the outer ridge, so as to facilitate their opening. Look at figure 8 [Plate 250]. These three uprights are held together by three pins made of a single piece [the tri-bolt], and positioned triangularly, which pass [through] the three uprights, outside of which they are riven, such that the uprights spread equally and form the seat. Look at figure 6, which represents the elevation, and figure 7, which represents the [plan view] closed as well as opened, where the ends of the uprights are lettered the same on the sides. Look also at figure 5, which represents the "echaudé" completely closed with the rivets of the pins, which are placed at 2 thumbs [outside of] the middle, so as to give more impalement [spread] to the seat. The top of this is nothing but a piece of leather or some sort of fabric attached at the end of the three uprights.

We also make campaign armchairs, which fold in their length, such that the two sides remain upright, having nothing but the crossbars in front and of the rear that break in two parts in the middle and are repelled from within. The crossbars of the backs also break in the middle, but on the edge. They come to be repelled on the edge of the crossbars. All these breaks are closed with some hinges, and are held in place with some hooks.

There are some armchairs where the break is not in the middle, but on the contrary is at the place of the leveling, which is much more neat, but demands more precautions for them to close well. There are others where the front, the back and the seat separate and enclose separately, and are reassembled really easily by means of hooks which are placed at the places of the joinery. I have not made drawings off these armchairs, because they appear to me to be useless, since what I just said being sufficient to facilitate their understanding.

Plate 251: Diagrams and Illustrations of a table and a camp bed with their Developments

We also make campaign tables, where the top and the leg break, and yet hold together [in one piece] to be easier to transport.

The top of these tables is composed of two pieces edged by [long]-grain wood, and joined together by tongue and groove, as represented in figures 2, 3 and 7. The leg of these tables is composed of four chassis which are attached two by two at both ends of the table, to which they are held with some hinges, noting to make it a bit shorter in thickness than the other. When they are folded, the bracket that you attach to the table in order to even out this difference in height, spreads to the second chassis of the table the thickness of the first, which, when folded, joins at the top. Look at figure 1, where the revolution of the first chassis *a-b* ends under the table at point *e*; and that of the second chassis *d-e*, ends on the second chassis at *f*. What I am saying for one side of the table should be understood for the other, as you can see in figure 5, which represents the table completely folded, and the chassis of the leg in its place and sides with the same letters as in the first figure.

Look also at figure 2, which represents the table viewed at the end with the spacer *g*, which serves to hold the legs apart, which is made of solid wood or [is] even joined, as in figure 6, so that it be lighter. We make still other campaign tables with clawfeet, like game tables and others, where the legs fold under them diago-

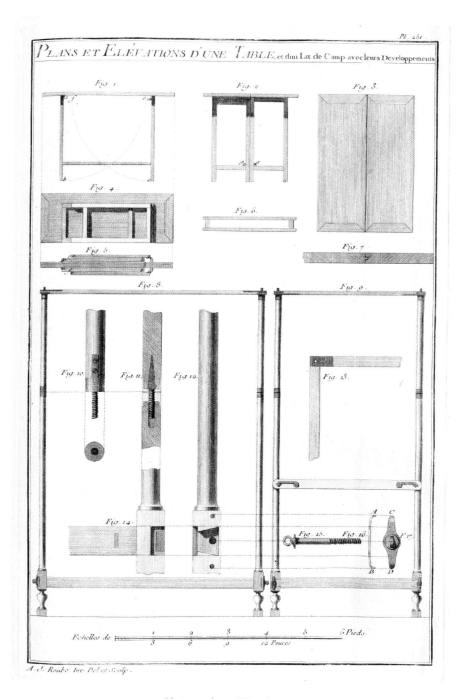

FIG. 5. Plate 251 from "l'Art du Menuisier."

nally, and are closed with some hinges, which you hold in place with some screws.

We also make night tables, some easy chairs and some bidets, of which the legs also fold beneath them, or relate to each other and are held with some screws, so that they are easier to transport, and their legs less subject to being broken, which happens often during transport, when either loading or unloading them. That's why we take the precaution of folding the legs, or removing them completely when they can be contained within, which is easy to do with commodes and bidets.

I am not going to extend myself any further on the subject of portable furniture, because what I have said is more than sufficient to be able to make all the styles and according to different needs. Besides which, they are less extensive in a camp or on a trip, than in the villages, where they seem to be reborn with the ability to satisfy all.

APPENDIX B
INDIA'S JOINERS

O wing to the primitive manner in which the Indian bungalows are built, the amount of inner woodwork which figures in their construction scarcely affords the colored joiner an opportunity of earning his living. Consequently he combines with his calling that of a cabinet-maker, and if he is asked to provide the frame for a chair, he loses little time in accepting the offer. In this connection, it may be added that except in the "hill stations" (where the cold climate is in favor of houses which are built upon the European plan) the bare, uncomfortable, one-storied bungalow meets with general approval. Doors, opening on to the veranda, take the place of windows; wainscotting is unknown, and if the rooms are provided with fire-places, the mantelpieces usually consist of a rough board which is coated with whitewash or distemper to match the walls. Fortunately for the joiner, tables, chairs and cupboards are required.

The "Aram Choki."

The article of furniture which is in the greatest demand is the "aram choki" – easy chair. It consists of a sloping back about four feet in length and a seat which is almost as long, and it stands about two and a half feet from the ground. The seat and back are cane, and one of the long arms has a small, circular piece taken out of it in order that the "Sahib" may place his tumbler of whisky-and-soda in the receptacle. These chairs usually are without any attempt at decoration; the legs seldom are turned, and the arms are severely straight and ugly. The dining-room chair, which faintly resembles a Chippendale model, has arms and is cane bottomed. It may be added that in the "plains" of India all chairs are cane-bottomed; the upholstered variety attracts so many mosquitos and other stinging insects, that to sit in them is little short of a penance.

Beds and Bedroom Furniture.

Although there is some demand for light French bedsteads, the native "charpoy" is by far the most popular. The "charpoy" consists of a rough frame across which is stretched a web-work of cord, or broad tapes. Upon this is placed a thin mattress – and it must be confessed that the tired exile sleeps as soundly on his rude couch as on the most expensive bed that ever left a New York furniture shop. The rest of the bedroom furniture which is made by the colored joiner and cabinetmaker includes a wash-hand stand, a chest of drawers, and an "almirah," or wardrobe. The wash-hand stand frequently consists of a single tripod, and the other articles decidedly are of the "penny plain" variety, being more or less devoid of any attempt at decoration. Occasionally, however, the black man is made happy by an order to make a decorative cabinet of the black, ebony-like wood, which is procurable in the north of India, while impecunious subalterns and other exiles, who desire to propitiate their well-to-do relations at "home," frequently commission Abdur Rahman to bring to the bungalow cunningly carved work-boxes of sandal wood inlaid with enamel and mother-o'pearl, "teak" writing desks, and boxes which are decorated with a labyrinth of Urdu characters. Nothing delights the native cabinet-maker more than to be invited to display his skill in this manner.

The Colored Joiner's Tools.

Except that the colored joiner's tools are roughly made and not always as sharp as might be desired, they scarcely differ from those which are used in civilized countries. But where labor-saving devices might be applied, he is strictly conservative. In fact, if he is employed – together with several other hands – in a manufactory, he looks upon these contrivances as inventions of the devil, designed to reduce the staff of workmen and to rob him of his only means of earning a living. Indeed, there is no rascality which he will not perpetrate to prejudice the proprietor against the use of machinery. He neglects to oil the bearings of fast running machinery, and when they become red-hot he chuckles in the sleeve of his voluminous eastern robe. The villain slashes the driving straps, breaks the cogs – in fact, there practically is no limit to his means toward an end. And if he is found out and punished, his supporters, to a man, go on strike.

Government Employ.

It is the aim and ambition of every native joiner and cabinet maker to obtain a government appointment. After serving five and twenty or thirty years in a government railway workshop or ship-building yard, he is entitled to a pension, and during his service he enjoys a social position which is far above that of the mere joiner who works on his own account. Indeed, so anxious is he to be a "sirkari noker" – government servant – that he willingly sacrifices a well-paid billet to secure the coveted appointment, even though it entails upon him commencing at the foot of the ladder and working his way upward. Eventually he may gain the position of foreman, a post which carries with it no little patronage, for all successful applicants for work make a point of handing over the greater part of the first month's pay to the grasping foreman. In this way, by the time he retires on his pension, he may be many hundreds of rupees to the good, an owner of house property, and a person of no little account in native circles.

Repairs.

Although a certain amount of furniture is made every year, the joiner and cabinetmaker owes a considerable portion of his income to the repairing orders which come his way. The average Anglo-Indian is a careful soul who grudges spending a single brass farthing more on his adopted country than he possibly can help. Consequently, instead of investing in new tables, chairs and cupboards, he much prefers to send the old ones to be mended. And if these are hopelessly damaged, rather than order new ones from the local store, he visits a second-hand "bazaar" shop – sending his purchases to be repaired. From time to time the dusky artisan tours the district, his paraphernalia being carried by a "coolie." He calls at the planters' indigo "concerns," or tea "gardens," and at the houses of the well-to-do natives. His enterprise, however, seldom meets with its reward. He tramps many a weary mile to earn a sum which scarcely would keep an American workman in beer and 'baccy for a week.

Camp Furniture.

The furniture to be found in a "bungalow" usually is made to fold up into a remarkably small space, so that when the nomadic Anglo-Indian official is suddenly transferred to another "station," his belongings can be packed into the smallest space. The wash-hand stand tripod takes up little more room than an umbrella, the tables are equally adaptable, and the wardrobe, being unpolished, can be used as a packing-case. Needless to add, the joiner community of the place for which the "Sahib" is bound pray that the furniture will sustain considerable damage en route, and that they may be invited to mend it.

Contentment.

Abdur Rahman is the happiest of mortals – a contented man. His earnings are comparatively small, sometimes miserably so, but he is satisfied with his lot. He may only receive the equivalent of a dollar for making a chest of drawers, consisting of three long drawers and two small ones, yet he blesses the day that brought him the order. Although he is paid a paltry "rupee" (32 cents) for furnishing a table with a new leg and double that sum for fitting it with a new leaf, he is thankful for small mercies. Two dollars and fifty cents – and find his own staining material and varnish – is the recognized price for making a wardrobe, and the man of color is deeply grateful to the white man who enables him to clear a profit of a dollar and a half on his work. It thus will be seen that his gains scarcely are colossal. On the other hand, the wind decidedly is tempered to the shorn lamb. He can lodge, feed and clothe himself for a yearly sum which works out at about six cents a day, while the upkeep of his wife is two-thirds of this figure. His children eat two cents' worth of food a day per child, and during the first half dozen years of their existence they wear few or no clothes – after which they earn their living. He requires no amusements, and when he is given a holiday he contentedly sleeps the scorching hours away. The payment of schooling fees does not trouble him, for, happily, in India the masses are not educated. Joiners and cabinet-makers have no use for reading, writing and other polite accomplishments. For generations past their forefathers have made chairs and cupboards – without being able to read a line of printed matter, and they rightly argue that there is no need for them to be better educated than their progenitors.

– By George Cecil, from *The Carpenter*, January 1910. *The Carpenter*, printed in Indianapolis, Ind., was the monthly journal of the United Brotherhood of Carpenters and Joiners of America. Reproduced here exactly as printed in the original newspaper.

ARMY & NAVY CO-OPERATIVE SOCIETY, LTD.,

105, VICTORIA STREET, WESTMINSTER, LONDON, S.W.

Telephone Nos.

Westminster, 461
(15 Lines).

Gerrard, 1892
(Box Office only).

Telegraphic Addresses:

" Army, London."
" Army, Plymouth."
" Army, Aldershot."
" Army, Portsmouth."
" Armistice, Bombay."
" Armistice, Calcutta."

The STORES are situated within Five Minutes' Walk of VICTORIA STATION, from which Omnibuses run to all parts of London.
The St. James's Park Station is within Three Minutes' Walk of, and is almost opposite the Stores.

RULES OF THE SOCIETY
AND
PRICE LIST
OF ARTICLES SOLD AT THE STORES.
No. 84.

15th MARCH, 1907.

LONDON:
PRINTED BY THE ARMY & NAVY CO-OPERATIVE SOCIETY, LIMITED, 105, VICTORIA STREET, WESTMINSTER, S.W.

FIG. 6. The Society's flagship store.

Front Rank, Firing Kneeling

APPENDIX C
ARMY & NAVY STORES

An overview of campaign furniture would be incomplete without discussing the Army & Navy Co-operative Society, Limited (later called the Army & Navy Stores). The massive department store was founded in 1871 by retired British officers who wanted to provide a supply of groceries to fellow officers at low prices.

The first store, a grocery, opened on Victoria Street in Westminster, London, in 1872 and quickly grew. Within a few years, the store added departments carrying stationary, drapes, clothing, furniture, firearms and tools, as well as a chemist (drugstore).

To join the Society and shop there you had to be an officer with your name published in the military's annual "Lists," or have one of the 11 other qualifications listed in the Society's membership rules, according to the company's 1907 catalog. These qualifications included, for example, being a widow or relative of an officer, serving in the Indian government or being a government official.

You also could join by being "introduced" to the Society by a current member; if the board of directors approved you, you were in.

Membership in the Society was desirable because the prices were lower than on the open market, and profits made by the store were returned to the shareholders.

In time, the Society opened manufacturing facilities to make its own campaign goods and opened depots in Bombay and Calcutta to serve customers there.

The Society published regular catalogs of its goods, which were 1,200-page doorstops filled with listings of tens of thousands of goods and prices, many of which could be delivered for free or almost free. The catalogs are a fascinating snapshot of British consumer culture in the late Victorian era and early 20th century, and they are regularly mined for information by academics and collectors.

For those interested in campaign furniture, the catalog is a useful pictorial guide to the different forms that were available, their dimensions and the materials used in their construction. The engravings, though small, are usually quite detailed; in many cases you can discern the hardware that was used on a particular piece.

During research for this book, I encountered several digitized copies of the catalog that were held by libraries, but the scans of those catalogs were coarse. So I purchased two original catalogs from English sources, one from 1907 and a second from 1929-30. The scans shown here were made at a high resolution so they could be reprinted larger than the originals' engravings, which were usually about an inch square.

In addition to the drawings, I have reprinted the items' descriptions and prices. I hope these images will give you some ideas for future pieces. Many of the furniture forms shown in the catalog are rarely found in museums or antique stores because they were designed to be used until they finally wore out.

The Society was acquired by House of Fraser, a department store chain founded in Glasgow. House of Fraser still operates a store at the Victoria Street location where the Society began and maintains an archive of materials relating to the Society, including price lists and other ephemera.

BOMBAY

CHESTS

No. 11. Chest of Aldershot pattern or Hut drawers, comprising one long and two small drawers, mounted on and packing into a printed deal case, as shown. Teak................ £6 13 0

Do. mahogany 6 15 6

Do. oak 6 11 9

No. 3a. Set of drawers, with table escritoire, but without shelves and fittings, size 3 ft. 3 in. long, 1 ft. 8 in. wide, 3 ft. 9 in. high. 2 drawers 5¾ in. deep, 1 drawer 7 in. deep, escritoire 4½ in. deep, 1 drawer 5¾ in. deep, 1 drawer 10½ in. deep. This chest is fitted with secret drawer. Teak £12 16 6

Do., oak 12 13 6

Do., mahogany 13 1 6

No. 8. With middle escritoire, 3 ft. 3
in. long, 1 ft. 7 in. wide, and 3 ft. 7
in. high ; secretary drawer 8¼ in.
deep, 2 small drawers 8¼ in. deep,
1 drawer 7¼ in. deep, 1 drawer 4¾
in. deep, 1 drawer 10½ in. deep.
Teak £10 13 9
Do., mahogany 10 18 3
Do., oak 10 6 6

No. 4. With deep centre drawer at top,
and two small drawers on either
side, size 3 ft. 9 in. long, 1 ft. 10 in.
wide, 3 ft. 10 in. high, 4 small
drawers 3¾ in. deep, 1 drawer 6½
in. deep, 1 ditto 10½ in deep, 2
drawers 8½ in. deep. Teak £11 2 9
Do., oak 10 13 3
Do., mahogany 11 8 0

No. 10.   Chest with long escritoire, 3 ft.
  3 in. long, 1 ft. 7 in. wide, 3 ft. 7 in.
  high, escritoire 8 in. deep.   One
  drawer 4½ in. deep, 1 drawer 8 in.
  deep, 1 drawer 10½ in. deep.   Teak £11 10 3
  Do., mahogany 11 10 3
  Do., oak 11 5 0

No. 4a.   Set of plain, 3 ft. 9. in. long,
  1 ft. 10 in. wide, 3 ft. 10 in. high, 2
  drawers 7½ in. deep, 1 drawer 10½
  in. deep, 2 drawers 8½ in. deep.
  Teak £9 16 9
  Do., mahogany 10 2 0
  Do., oak 9 9 9

No. 7.   Chest with side escritoire, 3 ft.
3 in. long. 1 ft. 6 in. wide, and 3 ft.
5 in. high, 2 drawers 8 in. deep, 1
drawer 7½ in. deep, 1 drawer 4 in.
deep, 1 drawer 10 in. deep.   Teak   £9 10 6
Do. mahogany 9 14 3
Do. oak 9 7 9

CHEST OF DRAWERS

To Order.

T.G.B. 4

3 ft. 3 in. long, 1 ft. 6 in. wide, and 3 ft. 5 in. high,
2 drawers 5 in. deep, 1 drawer 10 in. deep, 2 drawers
7 in. deep. Oak £20 0 0

Iron Bound and Painted Travelling Cases, with shelves
for above   ..   ..   .. per set £8 13 6

Cases for Chests of Drawers.

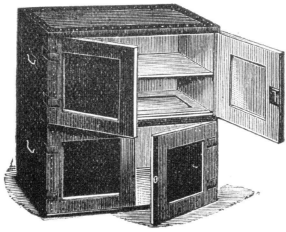

Cases for military chests of drawers, painted, iron bound, and fitted with sunk handles.

For Chests No. 2, 3, 4, and 4a.........	£4	14	9
,, ,, 3a	4	0	3
,, ,, 5 and 7...................	3	12	3
,, ,, 8, 9 and 10	3	14	6
,, ,, 5a (second quality), projecting handles	2	13	9

If with elm ends—

For Chests No. 2, 3, 4, and 4a.........	£5	0	6
,, ,, 3a	4	3	9
,, ,, 5 and 7...................	3	15	3
,, ,, 8, 9 and 10	3	18	0

If with elm ends and rounded corners—

For Chests No. 2, 3, 4, and 4a.........	£5	10	0
,, ,, 3a	4	13	6
,, ,, 5 and 7...................	4	5	3
,, ,, 8, 9 and 10	4	7	9

Any of the above sets of cases can be supplied fitted with brass rods, fittings and curtains to completely cover, extra.

In cretonne, complete	£1	5	0
,, art serge, ,, ...	1	7	0
,, repp, ,, ...	2	3	0

TRUNKS

Regulation Army Chests.

With sunk handles, as sealed pattern.

			Zinc lined.
1.	3 ft. 6 in. by 2 ft. 2 in. by 2 ft.	£3 5 9	£3 18 6
2.	3 ft. 4 in. by 1 ft. 10 in. by 1 ft. 8 in.	2 17 9	3 8 0
3.	2 ft. 6 in. by 2 ft. by 1 ft.	2 0 6	2 7 9
4.	2 ft. 2 in. by 1 ft. 2 in. by 1 ft.	1 8 3	1 13 0

Storage Boxes.

Outside stained and clamped with lock, and two countersunk screws in lid.

These boxes are designed to meet a demand for a strong but inexpensive chest, suited for travelling, storage of goods, plate, &c.

Outside measurement—	No. 1 size. 27 by 20½ by 16.	No. 2 size. 31 by 22½ by 19.	No. 3 size. 38 by 20 by 17½
Quite plain inside ...	21/0	23/9	27/6
Do., with wooden tray	25/6	29/0	34/9
Zinc lined	29/9	33/6	37/9
Do., with wooden tray	34/3	38/9	45/0
Green baize lined ...	30/6	35/0	38/6
Do., with wooden tray	42/6	47/0	50/3

No. 13. Strong Barrack Chest, iron bound and painted, to hold sundries, size 3 ft. by 1 ft. 8 in. by 1 ft. 8 in. £1 13 3

Do. do. lined with green baize and fitted with Bramah lock, for use as plate chest 2 19 3

Strong Chests for Travelling.
(Of good seasoned wood.)

No. 12.   Strong Sea Chest, 3 ft. by
    1 ft. 7 in. by 1 ft. 8 in., iron
    bound and painted £1 7 0
Fitted with a 6-in. tray 1 12 9

Zinc Lined Chests.
(Recommended for Officers' use and for India).

Zinc Lined, Approximately Air-tight, Sunk
Handles, a very strong box.

No. 1.   29 by 17½ by 18 in.} £2 10 6
 ,, 2.   32 ,, 17½ ,, 18 ,, ...   2 16 6
 ,, 3.   35 ,, 20½ ,, 21 ,,,, ...   3 8 0
 ,, 4.   38 ,, 20½ ,, 21 ,, ...   3 14 6

BEDS

Stretcher Bedstead.

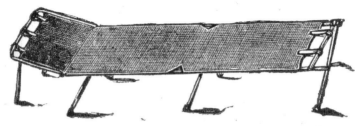

No. 69.   Strong portable camp or barrack
   stretcher bedstead, iron 42/9
   2nd quality do. 31/6
Black waterproof case to carry either of
   above bedsteads.............................. 15/3

Portable Wood Camp Bedstead.

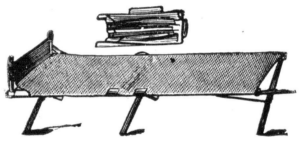

No. 71.   With iron clips and stays, and
   cavas bag to carry same 25/9
Do., do., size, 2 ft. 4 in. by 6 ft. 4 in. with
   extra strong clips, etc., and bag 39/3

The "Compactum" Camp Bed.

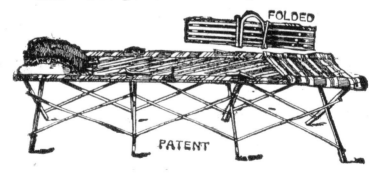

Cam ᐟ Fedstead.

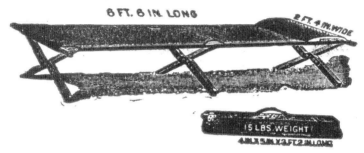

The Gold Medal Camp Bedstead (supply
uncertain) ....each 12/3

Improved Charpoy Bedstead.

(Registered design, 465534 and 465535.)

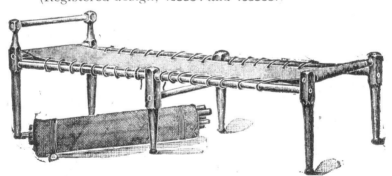

This has been designed by the Society with a
view to supplying a rigid bedstead, free from
hinges or bolts. Size, open 6 ft. 6 in. by 2 ft. 4 in.;
closed, 38 in. by 8½ by 7½. Weight about 25 lbs.
Ash frame, with green rot-proof sacking ... 32/0
Mosquito Rods............................extra 10/0
Green Bag, to hold bed and Rods 3/9

Lawes' Patent Combined Bed and Valise.

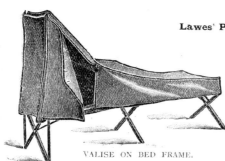

This invention consists of a valise, with fitted eyes, so as to be readily fixed to a frame, forming a combination of bedstead and field valise.

The frame is of ash throughout. Size 6 ft. 4 in. by 2 ft. 3 in. Weight approximately, 28 lbs. (Sticks for raising head extra).

Bed Frame 26/3
Valise, in green canvas 52/6
     ,, mail canvas 59/6

VALISE ON BED FRAME.

The Patent Trestle Hammock.
To order.

The Ash Trestles and connecting double cross-bar are made same as for Trestle Cot, and the hammock of strong canvas.

In bag complete, with stuffed pillow ... each 31/6.
Size when packed, 4 ft. long, 7 in. diameter.

The Columbia Bedstead.

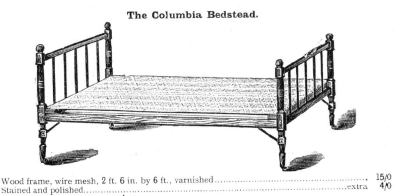

Wood frame, wire mesh, 2 ft. 6 in. by 6 ft., varnished.. 15/0
Stained and polished...extra 4/0

The Challenge Bedstead.

Similar in design to above folding spring bedstead, but with braided wire and end spiral spring
mattress.
2 by 6 ft. 11/9
2 ft. 6 in. by 6 ft. 13/0
2 ft. 6 in. by 6 ft. 4 in. 13/9
3 ft. by 6 ft. 4 in. 15/0

Howe's Patent Folding Crib.

No. 1, open.

	Wooden Lath Mattress.	Wire Mattress.
2 by 4 ft. stained and polished ...	15/2 ...	19/8
2 ft. 6 by 4 ft. 6 ,, ,, ...	16/4 ...	22/0

Mosquito rods extra, 2 ft. 5/0 ; 2 ft. 6 in. 5/8.

THE "X" IMPROVED COMPACTUM BED

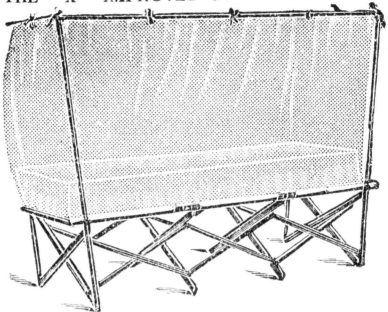

T.G.B. 16
6 ft. 6 in. long × 2 ft. 6 in. wide.

Bed, with Green Rotproof Canvas top, weight, 22 lb. (Mosquito Rods and Curtain extra) ..					58/-
Bed Bag, Green Rotproof Canvas, for above ..					5/6
A. & N. Mosquito Rods, for ditto, Wood				each	23/-
X	,,	,,	,,	,,	,,	14/6
X	,,	,,	,,	Brass	,,	9/-
A. & N.	,,	Net	,,	White	,,	20/-
X	,,	,,	,,	,,	,,	23/6
Quilted Kapok Mattresses, in Khaki ,, ..				,,	26/3
,, Hair	,,	G.R.C. ..		,,	26/3
,, Kapok	,,	,, ..		,,	25/6
,, ,,	,,	Green Sateen		,,	22/6
Hair Pillows, in G.R.C. ..	..	..		,,	5/9
Kapok ,,	,,	..	..	,,	4/9
,, ,, Khaki ..	..	..		,,	8/3
Cotton Sheets, 2 × 3 yd.	..	per pair			15/-
,, Pillow Cases	..	..	..	each	1/3

CHAIRS

Indian Chair.

Solid teak frame, cane seat and back, extending arms to use as leg rest...... 64/9
(Supply uncertain.)

No. 33.
Portable iron Douro Pattern Chair, with American cloth cushions and leg rest   80/9
Box for do. 30/3
Do., 2nd quality 25/9

Barrack Room Chairs.
(Showing cushion fitted on.)

Chairs only.
Oiled 5/6
Polished 6/0

No. 30.

Portable Douro Pattern Chair, with
    leather strap arms, horsehair
    cushions, covered with leather 69/9

Tapestry covers for do. ...... from 10/0

Box for above to form dressing
    table,   on   four legs, iron
    clamped and painted... .... 31/6

PORTABLE DIVAN CHAIRS.

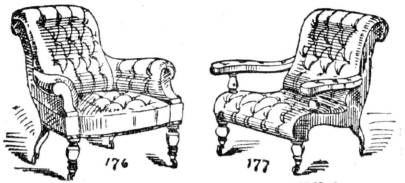

No. 176. Enclosed Arm Divan Chair, in roan, stuffed part hair £7 12 9
,, ,, Do. in moroco, all hair 9 0 9
No. 177. Do. Open Arm do. in roan, part hair 6 13 0
,, ,, Do. in morocco, all hair 8 4 9

The Bartlett Chair.
(Registered design.)

An improved form of Roorkee chair, it having a leg rest.

In ash, with white canvas seat and back...... 27/6
 Do., with extra high back 29/3
Bags to hold above 2/3

No. 26. Iron Folding Tent Chair 18/3
 Do., on castors 22/0

Roorkhee Folding Chair.

English make, of ash throughout, well finished.

Each 21/6

Do., in green canvas with back, to pack, extra short 24/3
Rough canvas bags for above chairs 2/3

Chairs and Stools.

C 2. Chair open.   Chair closed.

These open and close as easily as an umbrella, and are quite as portable.

	With iron corners.	Extra for gun metal corners.	Weight lb. oz.
Mark C 2 chair, extra strong	9/6	... 0/9	... 6 4½
,, C 4 large chair, extra strong ...	12/9	... 0/9	... 7 5½
,, C S stool, without backs	4/3	... 1/0	... 2 14½

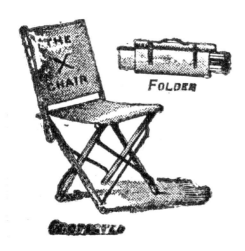

The "X" Chair.

Weight about 5 lb.

Striped material 4/2

Do., covered in
   green canvas 5/3

Lath Chair.

No. 14.

A comfortable chair in hardwood.

Polished 8/6

Stained and Polished walnut 10/0

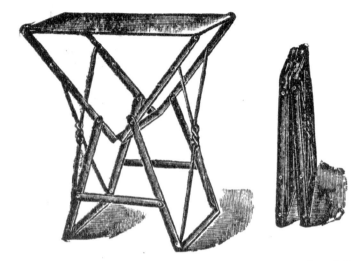

With iron frame and canvas seat ...... each 2/1

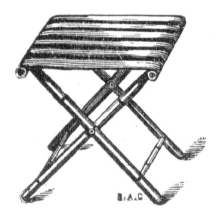

Canvas seat .... each 0/9½ 1/1
   „   „   with back .... each 1/4
Stronger pattern, hard wood frame, no back
                                        each 0/11½
Larger and stronger, hard wood frame, no
   back .... each 1/10 2/6

The Army & Navy Deck Chair.

Price 24/6

Cushion and lifebuoy, combined, covered in green rot-proof canvas, and stuffed with cork to fit this chair.................... 12/6

*Carrying Chair (C.)

Made of beech, French polished, caned back and seat 47/3
Packing for country, 3/6

THE IMPROVED ROORKHEE CHAIR
T.G.B. 91

With improved head rest, Green or Brown Canvas, Birch frame, in bag, **42/-**

Without head rest. Weight 10½ lb.
Price .. **34/-**

THE " VERDUN " FOLDING CHAIR

T.G.B. 89 Frame made of selected Hardwood, with Japanned fittings. Seat of Green Rot-proof Canvas. Weight, 7 lb.

Price each **13/9**

DESKS

THE "PRINCESS" FOLDING WRITING TABLE.

With self-righting sliding stationery rack, containing nickel-plated frame to hold post and date cards. The table is fitted with 2 plated letter clips, safety ink penholder, pencil, scissors, and penknife.

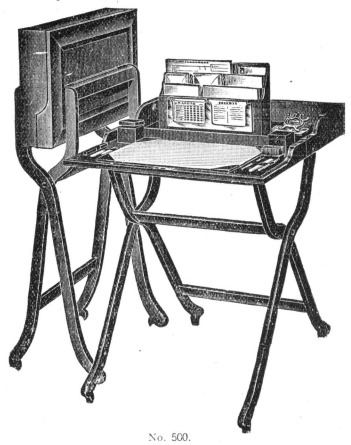

No. 500.

Oak	£6	15	0
Mahogany	7	2	6

THE "QUEEN" PATENT TURNOVER AND EXTENDING WRITING TABLE.

Polished Walnut, fitted complete £9 10 0
  ,,   Mahogany 10 7 6
  ,,   ,,   Inlaid Marqueterie 11 18 6

The "Alliance."

Imitation Persian—

	10½	12	14	16 in.
Unfitted	22/6	26/6	29/6	33/0
Do., fitted	26/9	31/0	34/0	38/6

WALNUT WOOD WRITING TABLE.

Walnut Wood, with leather covered top and fittings; pockets for various sizes note paper and envelopes, post cards, large pocket for loose letters, fitted with safety ink, perpetual calendar, pen, pencil, scissors, penknife, paper knife, and memorandum slate.

Size when open, 28 in. high, top, 21 in. square 87/0
Green Oak, do. do. do. 87/0

The "Harrow" Writing Desk.

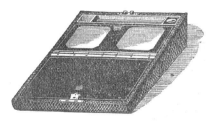

Long grain polished 'roan leather, size
  12 by 8¼ by 4 in. 8/9
Do., do., diced Persian leather, size 12 by
  8¼ by 4 in. 10/9

FOLDING TYPEWRITING TABLE
(Also for Writing Table.)

It occupies very little room when folded. It is very light and can be easily carried to any part of the room. The partitions and drawer hold writing paper and carbons for typewriting, also letters, etc.
And all papers are private when the table is closed.
Registered No. 742723. ..   ..   ..   54/- each.

The "Winchester" Desk.

Polished roan leather, recess for papers in slope, fitted complete, lock and key, 14 in. 22/6

TABLES

Table. Mark C.T.

These tables are quite firm and steady, the top rolls up, and the frame folds as shown.
Size, 36 in. square.

With iron corners .... each 17/6
Extra for gun metal corners .... ,, 1/2
Weight 12 lb.
N.B.—The above Paragon Furniture will take from three to six days to procure.

Camp Tables.

No. 67. No. 68

No. 67. Portable Camp Table, 24 by 18 in. 12/9
,, ,, ,, 30 ,, 20 ,, 15/0
,, ,, ,, 36 ,, 21 ,, 16/8

The Patent "X" Table.

Folding, size of top 24 in. by 19 in............ 6/7
Do., top covered green canvas ,................ 8/6
Do., size of top 32 in. by 26 in., top covered
green canvas 15/0

The Lennox Portable Tables.

(Patented by the late Lieutenant-General Sir
Wilbraham Lennox, V.C., K.C.B., R.E.)

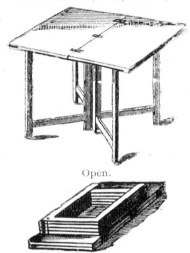

Open.

Closed.

Suitable for picnics, gardens, races, or camp.
The table consists of two pieces only, viz., the top,
which folds up, and the legs, which are hinged
together. The legs are arranged diagonally, so
that persons sitting at the four sides are not inter-
fered with by any woodwork. Size of table 3 ft.
square, weight about 25½ lb., and packs in a space
of 3 ft. by 1½ ft. by 6 in.

Price.. 35/0
Do., new pattern, so arranged that a side
    may be placed flat against the wall 51/6

Folding Card Table.

No. 64,

Green baize top with stained and polished (walnut)
    tapered legs, improved pattern and very rigid.

24 in. square 19/3
27   ,, ... 20/0
30   ,, ... 20/6

Folding Dining Table.

To order only.

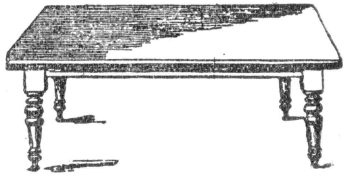

Basswood tops, birch legs, 3 ft. by 3 ft. 30/6

„   „   „   „   4 „   2 ft. 6 in 28/9

„   „   „   „   6 „   3 ft. 42/0

Intermediate and larger sizes can be procured.

The Explorer's Table.

Specially recommended for African use. Size about 40 in. by 23 in., height, 26½ in. Very rigid when erected.

Price 22/6

„   second quality 18/3

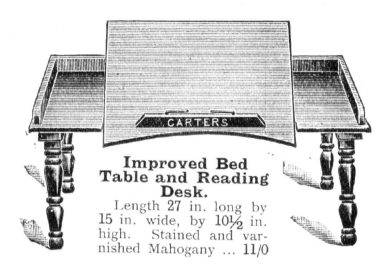

Improved Bed Table and Reading Desk.

Length 27 in. long by 15 in. wide, by 10½ in. high. Stained and varnished Mahogany ... 11/0

THE "VELOCK" FOLDING CARD TABLE.

Fumed Oak, with panelled cloth top, size 28 in. by 28 in. .... each 14/6

**THE
" MAITLAND "
FOLDING
PATIENCE,
PIQUET AND
PLAYING
CARD TABLE.**

Polished walnut,
   lined cloth ... 53/6

OTHER STORAGE

Towel Horse.

No. 61.

No. 61. Towel Horse, teak, mahogany, or
   oak.. 10/6

No. 62. With double rail at top 14/6

Boot Racks.
(Supply uncertain).

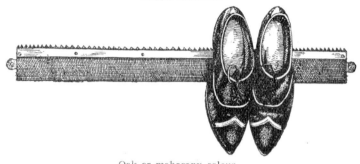

Oak or mahogany colour.

18 in.	1/7½
21 „	1/9½
24 „	1/11½

Boot Racks and Stands.

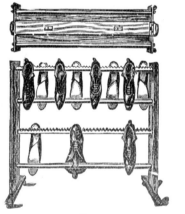
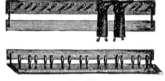

No. 30.

No. 27.   No. 32.

No. 27.	Boot Stand		15/9
„ 30.	Cavalry Top Boot Rack	7/6	11/0
„ 32.	Boot and Shoe Rack, 2 ft. long		6/3
„ „ „ „ „ 3 „			7/6
Telescope Curtain Rod with rings and brackets complete			12/0

The "Securem" Tent Pole Strap.

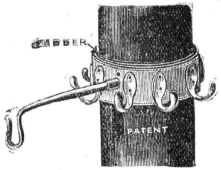

This strap, lined with corrugated rubber, adheres closely to the pole, and so does not slip when articles are hung on it, the hooks being short and strong do not bend. Besides serving military purposes, it will be found useful in bathing and cricket tents.

8 hooks and lantern holder.................... 5/0
8   „   without lantern holder............ .... 3/10

CAMP EQUIPMENT—contd.

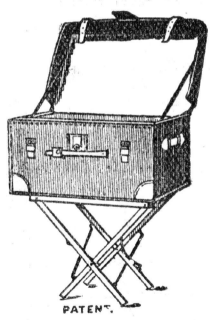

PATENT.

FOLDED

The "X" Folding Luggage Stand.

This stand is exceedingly strong and will carry the weight of a heavy trunk, can be instantaneously folded and packed inside the trunk, thus the traveller is never without a luggage stand.

Size folded, 24 in. long, by 3½ in. by 1 in., 2/10

22.nd F'r Bayonets.

ACKNOWLEDGEMENTS

The following people were invaluable in the production of this book. Without their help, this book would be far more boring, less picturesque, incomplete or just wrong.

Nancy Andersen, Londonderry Brasses
Ty Black
Jeff Burks
John Cashman
Sean Clarke, Christopher Clarke Antiques
Simon Clarke, Christopher Clarke Antiques
Richard Dabb, National Army Museum
Suzanne Ellison
Mark Firley
Megan Fitzpatrick
Orion Henderson, Horton Brasses
Greg Miller
Mike Siemsen

Front Rank Kneeling

Front Rank, Firing Kneeling

FURTHER READING

Army & Navy Co-operative Society Ltd. Price List 1907. London: Army & Navy Co-operative Society Ltd., 1907. Print.

Army & Navy Co-operative Society Ltd. Price List 1929-30. London: Army & Navy Co-operative Society Ltd., 1929. Print.

Bade, Stanley. *Colonial Furniture in New Zealand*. Wellington: Reed, 1971. Print.

Bellew, Francis John. *Memoirs of a griffin; or, A cadet's first year in India*. London: W.H. Allen, 1843. Print.

Bowett, Adam. *Woods in British Furniture-making, 1400-1900: An illustrated historical dictionary*. Wetherby: Oblong Creative, 2012. Print.

Brawer, Nicholas. "Georgian Campaign Furniture." *The Magazine Antiques*. June 2000: 924-931. Print.

Brawer, Nicholas. *Britain's Portable Empire*. Katonah, New York: Katonah Museum of Art, 2001. Print.

Brawer, Nicholas. *British Campaign Furniture: Elegance Under Canvas, 1740-*

1914. New York: Harry N. Abrams, 2001. Print.

Cecil, George. "India's Colored Joiners." *The Carpenter*. Jan. 1910: 44-46. Print.

Clarke, Sean, and Simon Clarke. *The Portable Empire*. Gloucestershire: Christopher Clarke (Antiques) Ltd., 2003. Print.

Clarke, Sean, and Simon Clarke. *Essential Baggage*. Gloucestershire: Christopher Clarke (Antiques) Ltd., 2004. Print.

Clarke, Sean, and Simon Clarke. *An Englishman's Tent*. Gloucestershire: Christopher Clarke (Antiques) Ltd., 2005. Print.

Clarke, Sean, and Simon Clarke. *England Expects*. Gloucestershire: Christopher Clarke (Antiques) Ltd., 2005. Print.

Clarke, Sean, and Simon Clarke. *Furniture Fit for Heroes*. Gloucestershire: Christopher Clarke (Antiques) Ltd., 2006. Print.

Clarke, Sean, and Simon Clarke. *Brass Bound & Portable*. Gloucestershire: Christopher Clarke (Antiques) Ltd., 2007. Print.

Clarke, Sean, and Simon Clarke. *The Captain's Kit Bag*. Gloucestershire: Christopher Clarke (Antiques) Ltd., 2007. Print.

Clarke, Sean, and Simon Clarke. *The Quartermaster General*. Gloucestershire: Christopher Clarke (Antiques) Ltd., 2008. Print.

Clarke, Sean, and Simon Clarke. *For King, Country & Comfort*. Gloucestershire: Christopher Clarke (Antiques) Ltd., 2009. Print.

Clarke, Sean, and Simon Clarke. *The Great Escape*. Gloucestershire: Christopher Clarke (Antiques) Ltd., 2009. Print.

Clarke, Sean, and Simon Clarke. *First Class Travel*. Gloucestershire: Christopher Clarke (Antiques) Ltd., 2010. Print.

Clarke, Sean, and Simon Clarke. *Lieutenant Wilmot's Bungalow*. Gloucestershire: Christopher Clarke (Antiques) Ltd., 2011. Print.

Clarke, Sean, and Simon Clarke. *My Barrack Room*. Gloucestershire: Christopher Clarke (Antiques) Ltd., 2012. Print.

Clarke, Sean, and Simon Clarke. *Flying the Flag*. Gloucestershire: Christopher Clarke (Antiques) Ltd., 2013. Print.

Clarke, Sean, and Simon Clarke. *Rule Britannia*. Gloucestershire: Christopher Clarke (Antiques) Ltd., 2013. Print.

Joy, Edward T. *English Furniture 1800-1851*. London: Sotheby Parke Bernet Publications, 1977. Print.

Kephart, Horace. *Camping and Woodcraft: A Handbook for Vacation Campers and for Travelers in the Wilderness*. New York: Outing Publishing, 1916. Print.

Munday, John. "Captains and Cabins." *The Connoisseur*. Feb. 1979: 90-97. Print.

Phillips, Jerome. "Travelling and Campaigning Furniture 1790-1850." *Antique Collecting*. June 1984: 7-11. Print.

Phillips, Jerome. "Furniture for Travel 1760-1860." *Antique Collecting*. June 1987: 38-43. Print.

Rieder, William. "Antiques: Campaign Furniture." *Architectural Digest*. July 1995: 102-106, 140. Print.

Rosoman, Treve. "Military Furniture." *Antique Collecting*. Apr. 1985: 44-46. Print.

Subaltern, A. "Sketches of Burmah." *The Asiatic journal and monthly register for British and foreign India, China and Australasia* 26. July-December (1828): 548. Print.

Fig. 6. "The Tiger Hunt" (detail),
Brain & Payne, 12 Paternoster Road
(London).

17th Take up Firelock.

INDEX

Army & Navy Co-operative Society, 11, 13, 45, 155, 284-286, *287-317*

B

bastard grain and table legs, *217*, 220
beds, *268*, 270-275, *277*, 280, *294-298*
    Army & Navy Stores catalog, *294-298*
    Roubo's lit de campaign, *268*, 270-275, 277
Black, Ty, 158
bookcase, 249, 250-263
    build a traveling bookcase, 249-263
        carcase, 250-255, 256
        cutlist, 250
        drawers, 258-261
        interior finish, 261-263
        lock, 255, 257-258
bookshelves, 235-247
    build collapsible bookshelves, 240-247

cutlist, 240
shelves, 243-247
uprights, 241-243
boot racks, 316
Bowett, Adam: "Woods in British Furniture-Making 1400-1900,"
40, 42, 45, 47, 319
brasses, *see* hardware
Brawer, Nicholas A., viii, 4, 8, 319

C

campaign furniture
dating, 3, 15-16
development of lighter pieces, 11, 13
earlier styles, 2, 4, 6, 7
field guide to, 15-37
origins, viii, 1-3
20th century, 13
versatility, viii
Victorian era, 5, 9-12, 14
camp stool, 138-153, *273*, 275-276
build a folding camp stool, 141-152
cutlist, 142
leather seat, 144, 148-150, 152
legs, 141-148, 151
materials, 139-142, 153
three-way bolt, 147-148, 153
Roubo's echaudés, *273*, 275-276
chairs
aram choki, 279-280
Army & Navy Stores catalog, *299-306*
Douro, 32, *299, 300*
field guide to, 30-37
folding, *x*, 30-32
patent, *8*
Roubo's folding chair, *273*, 275, 276
Roorkhee
Army & Navy Stores catalog, *301, 302, 306*
build the 1898 version, 157-158, 160-186
cutlist, 160
finish, 174-175
leatherwork, 162, 176-186

      legs, 161-171
      material selection, 157-158, 161
      stretchers, 172-174
   1898 chair, 156-157
   field guide to, 33-37
   history, 13, 155
   influence on modern design, 36-37, 156
   taller version, 159
  Safari, 36, 156, 188-189
chests
  Army & Navy Stores catalog, *287-290*
  build a campaign chest, 87-121
    base and feet, 108-111
    brasses, 112-119
    cutlist, 88
    drawer arrangement, 83-87
    finish, 120-121
    joinery, 91-108
  field guide to, 15-23
  navy vs. army, 22-23
  origins, 3
  packing cases for, 3, 22, 23, *291*
  period examples, *4-7*, 14
Christopher Clarke Antiques, 3
Clarke, Sean, 3, 11, 21-22, 49, 320, 321
Clarke, Simon, 3, 49, 320, 321

desks, *x*, 214-233, *307-310*
  Army & Navy Stores catalog, *307-310*
  build a folding field desk, 217-233
    apron, 222-230
    cutlist, 218
    legs, *217*, 220-222
    top, 231-232
  Douro. *See under* chairs

end grain gluing, 197, *199*

F

filing jig, 204, *205*
French campaign furniture, 32, 268-278

G

glue failure, 11
grain run-out, 157-158

H

hammock, 276
hardware
    flush vs. surface-mounted, 10-11, *63*, 64
    installing
        corner brackets, 64-70, 112-114
            with router, 69-70
        corner guards, 10, 11, 71-73, 115-117, 207-208, *209*
            hammer helper, *210*
        hinges, 132-133, 216, 226-231, *232*, 242-246
        lifts, 26, 117, *120*
        locks, 81, 255, 257-258
        pulls, 10, 15, *52*, 73-81, 117-119, 259-261
            router template for, 75-76
            skeletonized, 10, *52*, 76, 78-81
        secretary drawer quadrant stays, 133-134
    manufacturing methods, 54-62
    selecting, 62-63
    screws, 63, 92
    sources for, 331-332
    stripping zinc from, 148, 187
    three-way bolts for camp stools, 147-148, 153
    Victorian era, 10

I

'India's Joiners,' 279-282

K

Klint, Kaare, 36, 156. *See also* Safari: chairs

L

lap desks. *See* writing slopes
leatherwork. *See under* camp stool or Roorkee: chairs

luggage stand, *317*

metamorphic furniture. *See* patent furniture
Miller, Greg, 179-180

patent furniture, vii, 8-9

rivet joinery for trunks, 192-193
Roorkee chair. *See under* chairs
Roubo's campaign furniture, 268-278

Safari chair. *See under* chairs
secretaries, *6, 7*, 22-23, 122-137
    build a secretary, 123-137
        cutlist, 128
        drawer arrangement, 123-126
        drawer tape, 136
        finishing, 137
        gallery, 126-129, 135-136
        joinery, 130-133, 135-137
        quadrant stays, 133-134
    field guide to, 22-23
Siemsen, Mike 153

tables, 276, *277*, 311-315
    Army & Navy Stores catalog, *311-315*
    Roubo's table de camp, 276, *277*
tent pole strap, 317
towel horse, 315
trunks, *vi, x*, 24-27, 190-213, *292-293*
    Army & Navy Stores catalog, *292-293*
    build a strong trunk, 193-213
        assembly, 197-198,
        brass-screw rivets, 192, 201, 203-206
            filing jig, 204-205
        corner brasses, 207-209

cutlist, 194
feet, 208, 210-212, 213
finishing, 212
joinery, 193-197
seal, 198, 201-202
field guide to, 24-27
lifts for, 26, 117, *120*

wallpaper for a bookcase, 261-263
woods in campaign furniture, 38-51, *266-267*
ash (*Fraxinus* spp.), 40, 49
camphor (*Cinnamomum* spp.), *38*, 40, 47
mahogany (*Swietenia* spp.), 39, *41*, 41-43
oak (*Quercus* spp.), 40, *48*, 48, 49
substitues for exotic woods, 40, 266-267
teak (*Tectona grandis*), 40, *44*, 44-47, 92, 121
finishing, 121
gluing, 47, 226
working with, 46, *92*
walnut (*Juglans* spp.), 40, 49-51
writing slopes, 28-29, *308, 309, 310*

Zimmerman, Dale, 197

Fig. 6. Vintage campaign brasses
purchased from eBay.

Front Rank, Firing Kneeling

Front Rank, Kneeling

HARDWARE SOURCES

C ampaign brasses are sold by many vendors, both in the United States and England. The hardware is not always labeled "campaign hardware," however, and all the pieces might not be grouped together in the catalog.

In addition to looking for your hardware in catalogs, it also pays to search for campaign brasses on eBay and through other sellers of secondhand junk. Campaign brasses have been in continuous production since the 18th century. There is a lot of stuff out there if you are willing to look. The following is a list of hardware suppliers I have used when building campaign pieces. It is by no means exhaustive.

Ansaldi & Sons
29 Sullivan Road, Hudson, NH 03051
877-686-7201
ansaldi.com

Horton Brasses Inc.
49 Nooks Hill Road, Cromwell, CT 06416
800-754-9127
horton-brasses.com

Lee Valley Tools
P.O. Box 1780, Ogdensburg, NY 13669
800-871-8158
leevalley.com

P.O. Box 6295, Station J, Ottawa, ON K2A 1T4
800-267-8767
leevalley.com

Londonderry Brasses Ltd.
P.O. Box 415, Cochranville, PA 19330
610-593-6239
londonderry-brasses.com

Optimum Brasses Ltd.
Unit 1, Upstairs, Global Park, Station Road, Bampton, Devon EX16 9NG
+44 (0) 1398 331515
optimumbrasses.co.uk

Van Dyke's Restorers
P.O. Box 52, Louisiana, MO 63353
800-558-1234
vandykes.com

Whitechapel Ltd.
P.O. Box 11719, Jackson, WY 83002
800-468-5534
whitechapel-ltd.com